MW00801037

Awareness
Is Everything

Awareness
Is Everything

Why Wait?

Gretchen Sortzi

M.A.D. Hawk Productions
6359 Stanford Court
Mechanicsburg PA 17050

Copyright © 2014 Gretchen Sortzi. All rights reserved.

No part of this publication may be reproduced or
transmitted in any form or by any means, electronic
or mechanical, including photocopying, recording or
any other information storage and retrieval system,
without the written permission of the author.

Book interior design by Church Road Books
www.churchroadbooks.com
Cover art by Kathy Dill

ISBN-13: 978-1502479037
ISBN-10: 1502479036

PRINTED IN THE UNITED STATES OF AMERICA

For Kathleen L. Russell, whose love and wisdom brought my soul into consciousness, provided endless knowledge and gave me a voice. I wrote this book two years ago with your inspiration. I miss you every day. Heaven is so lucky to have you.

What were you before? Probably closer to a constant numbness, happy enough but not oozing the crazy euphoric feeling. You saw each day come and go. Now days feel like weeks as you see beyond this dull reality around you. The positive energy we create with this new thinking increases our production of divine energy.
— Gretchen Sortzi

It's amazing how you can live the same life, work at the same job, live in the same house, but feel SO different.
— Jen Neusbaum

Contents

Exercises And Meditations

Preface

I grew up in an extremely religious home. The daughter of devout Christians, I learned most of life's lessons through the Bible. In the last decade, I have spent a lot of time getting closer to God and studying many different avenues of spiritual growth. Our Source, our God, wants blessings for us and I consider myself to be an extremely spiritual person now. I still enjoy the lessons and morals the Bible provides. It includes great stories to lift us up and remind us of the power within all of us.

I remember the story of Jonah as one of my childhood favorites. This story was about a man who received a calling to do God's work. He ignored this calling and ran from his destiny. He experienced grave consequences until he gave in and did what was on his heart.

I always felt like I could relate to Jonah. I knew I had great potential. More importantly, I knew I felt called to important things and intense passions, but I also knew I was afraid and often just didn't want to. I have been running from my true calling for a long time. I've jumped on and off the wagon, battling my way there. I have been so close to the right path at some points in my life that things moved like true magic.

In 2004, miracles began to happen in my life every day and the road to everything I had ever dreamed of opened up before my very eyes. I had 6 fabulously successful health clubs, a beautifully furnished home for my daughter and me with a full-time nanny for her, and the ability to spread blessings to anything and anyone I wanted. I could make someone's car payment without blinking and I did. I founded a charity for abused women, taking in a very young staff member and treating her as my own. She lived with me and I provided everything she needed, wanting only her love in return. She is still an important member of my family.

I reached a point in my early 20s that most people don't reach until their 50s or beyond. I had complete financial freedom with a tall order of responsibilities to match. I was making a mark on the world — the mark I was being called to make. My speaking presentations and knowledge of my brand was outstanding. I was growing by leaps and bounds.

At the height of my success in 2005, I acquired a corporate job with our parent company and I was on top of the world. Every aspect of my life was ticking along in the perfect clockwork motion. Everything was working like magic and I believed I could handle it all. As the training period passed and I settled into my new job, balancing 6 businesses and my daughter began to be quite a challenge. I did my best to keep up with it all, but feelings of doubt started creeping into my mind. I began to feel inadequate and unable to manage everything. Thoughts of failure led to even more negative feelings. I felt guilty if I wasn't with my daughter. I felt guilty if I was working for one job and not the other.

The rush of thoughts and feelings grew worse and worse each day. Being a single mom added a lot of pressure too. I wanted to provide the best for my daughter, all the things I didn't have growing up, but both sides of that coin had consequences. Soon, I was traveling so much that I barely got to see her. I tried to take her on the road as much as I could, but that just made my job more difficult. I started to resent my job and myself.

To add salt to the wound, my superior's kind disposition upon introduction was not reality and often I ended phone calls with her in tears. She was terminated for the way she treated everyone on my team, but that didn't change what had already happened. Her condescending tone and constant harsh words left terrible thoughts and feelings spiraling through my head. As I began to doubt my ability to do the job, I saw a decline in my ability to manage the stress and the workload. I created movies in my mind of losing everything and I pushed "play" over and over. I had feelings of loss and inadequacy and my behaviors began to express things that did not serve my highest self. I desired negative activities and gravitated towards negative people. I enjoyed others who would sit with me and stew over all the loss, all the pain, all the wrongs around me. I became a victim caught in the vortex of negative energy and I easily created negative consequences.

The pressure from my boss led me to make several bad decisions. At one of our conferences, I was so messed up from an encounter with her that I walked out. I could not manage the conflicts and feelings in my mind, and I got a terrible migraine. I felt so much guilt from not being able to meet my boss's unrealistic expectations and being so far from home that I simply could not manage it all. I changed my flight and went home early without telling anyone. I truly couldn't handle the negative thoughts and feelings for another moment.

I was called on several occasions to quit that job and I didn't listen. I wanted that job, the success, the notoriety of it. I had dreamed of this title since I bought my first club and frankly, I felt born to do it. I inspire people and that was the main function of this job. I was in the spotlight and I loved that too. God wanted me to quit but I resisted. It wasn't long until the team was dissolved one by one. I was the first person to be let go on my team. God saw to it that I got out of this negative vortex that continued to bring me further down.

By the time I returned to working for my 6 health clubs, they had seen a major reduction in profit. There was not enough money to pay me and the loss of my other job made this season extremely scary for me. I had to let my daughter's nanny go and take staff hours at one of our clubs. My thoughts of failure and loss grew worse and worse until they were all I could think about. I dove deeper into negative relationships and found myself chasing after betrayal, devastation and addiction. I was tortured by day in my mind and by night in my dreams.

My debt continued to climb as the economy continued to decline. With a 75% pay cut for me, I began living off my credit cards to pay for basic needs. I ran every card I had to the max. My house quickly went into foreclosure.

During this time, I was receiving specific messages about my mind and my behaviors. Referrals to books and seminars, programs that fostered learning and inspiration, friends who were the kind I needed, all just showed up. And yet, I stayed in misery, kicking and screaming.

I received messages for over a year to put my house up for sale and move. It was beyond clear. I didn't see a way and I just wouldn't let go and believe. I was filled with fear and rebellion. I loved my house.

I received messages on numerous occasions to leave my addictions alone. It was beyond clear. I didn't see a way to let them go, so I just held on tight. I was filled with fear and rebellion. I enjoyed these behaviors.

I received messages on numerous occasions to end damaging relationships and change my circle of influence. I ignored every sign and blatantly said "no." I fought tooth and nail like a teenager. I was selfish, self-indulgent and completely out of control.

I had lost my own ability to move. I was trapped in a negative spiral that was moving so fast I had no idea how to turn it around. I continued to ignore the messages, the signs all around me. Many people would be in awe of just how clear God was with me. The path was laid at my feet, but I would not take a step.

I scrambled in all sorts of areas to make whatever money I could, all while digging a deeper and deeper hole. I couldn't put distance between relationships in my life where it was needed. I was surrounded by destructive people, havoc in the world around me. I got caught up so deep that I was living a life of misery, and the pain and heartache just kept mounting. I held hands with darkness. I lay down with sorrow and woke to suffering.

I started to yearn for my life to change, for the pain to stop. I started imagining all the good that I wanted for myself. Over the course of a year, people, both negative and positive, began to line up in my life as God desired, one by one. I spent months in constant awe just shaking my head at the divine journey lined up before me. The light at the end of the tunnel shone again and I could finally see a way out. I continued to learn and read, to open my awareness to knowledge that could help me grow. I started to pay attention to people and my surroundings, becoming aware of what was influencing me. I discovered what joy was and that I could find it without the addictions I believed I needed. I could see life through a new set of lenses and the euphoria was far beyond that of my negative experience.

Although my awareness continued to open, I struggled sometimes to see the blessings through the extreme changes that began to occur within my life.

I lost my house to the bank. That put me on my knees but after some grieving, I gave in completely to the calling and the opportunities ahead. It was the moment I knew things were changing and only faith would get me through. I was forced to move into my mother's basement. I had to use food stamps to eat. I dislocated both of my feet. I had to work so hard to stay in faith that there were days I didn't know where to pull it from. One day I was outside, lying in the grass and meditating. I could hear a voice speaking to me, "Be strong and let the old fall away. Be strong and let the old fall away." I heard it over and over in my mind. When I stood up, I knew I wanted more for my life and I was giving in completely. That moment, I knew I was being called to do something powerful with my lessons in life. Faith took over and a fearless woman stood up, ready to remain faithful and happy.

Losing my house was all part of God's plan, as was everything else that went on. It enabled me to give up my addictions to negative people and things. It enabled me to relocate to where I was supposed to be. It started a chain of reactions that changed my life.

I'm not perfect by any means. I have a long way to go. But the journey I have begun is an amazing transformation. I've learned to apply some simple fundamentals to my life and the result is life changing. I expect to learn forever on these subjects and always push for more information. I believe Awareness is Everything. The more aware I become, the stronger I get.

I do not view my past as a series of mistakes, but instead look at every negative choice, behavior and consequence as a lesson from which I chose to learn and become stronger. I will share with you some of my experiences and lessons as we go.

But this book isn't about me. It's about you! And it's about how the lessons I have learned are lessons for all of us to live by today. We all know what it feels like to be Jonah, waiting to grow up and accept our divine calling.

God has placed a great desire on my heart to share that information with others. I ask only that His will be done. I was one of the greatest "waiters" I know. I implore you to stop waiting, stop running, stop hiding from all the blessings that are yours. Open your eyes to a new world and a new life. It only takes a spark to light a fire. You can change everything in your reality right now.

Once I learned to change my thoughts, my feelings and my behaviors and gave into faith and expecting greatness, things turned around so fast. The assignment God placed in my heart to write books and speak this message is unfolding before my very eyes into a glorious victory. I want blessings for you *right now*.

Acknowledgements

Over the past 15 years I have battled anorexia, compulsive eating, drug and alcohol addictions and forged through damaging and abusive relationships. I have many people to thank who have walked with me along this journey to this place of freedom and opened my eyes to just how powerful and amazing life can be.

First, to my dear mother Joyce. Thank you for teaching me to love everyone unconditionally, from the inside out. Thank you for being an example of what this kind of love is all about and teaching me to be the kind of mother you were to us. Thank you for your endless understanding, your tremendous heart and your infinite wisdom. My world is brighter because of you.

I have heard many times that it takes a village to raise a child and I've seen that in my own life. A huge thank you to my aunts, who loved me as their own and lead a life of courage, strength and personal victory I admire so much. Aunt Diane, She-She, Brenda Brenda, Betty and Debbie, my world is brighter because of you.

To my best friends, who have loved me in my darkest times, I give you endless thanks. To Jen, I thank God every day that he brought you into my life. The joy we experience together is something I have longed for. You are one of my greatest gifts and I am in awe of how amazing you are. My world is brighter because of you.

To Jules, I thank God every day that He brought you into my life. You have been my rock in so many times of struggle and have loved me despite my lowest moments. You truly get me and who I am and have loved me in times I thought no one else did. My world is brighter because of you.

To my Linda, I thank God every day that He brought you into my life. You are not only a dear friend, but a mother, sister and soul mate. You can actually see and feel through my eyes and it is something I truly cherish. My world is brighter because of you.

To my Daijon "Meese", I thank God every day that He brought you into my life. You are like my own and I treasure the time in our lives we spent together. Watching you grow up was a true blessing for me. My world is brighter because of you.

To all the ladies I have met over the last 15 years in my profession, I am forever grateful for the many lessons you have shared with me and your love as you watched me grow. You are all my aunts, my grandmas and my friends. My world is brighter because of you.

To Gary and Diane Heavin for calling me out so many years ago and holding my hand as I started my journey of self-discovery and learned to love my own body. My world is brighter because of you.

To Bethany, Steve and Leslie who gave so much of their time and talent to make this book possible. I am forever in debt to all of you for your hard work and your empowering attitudes through it all. My world is brighter because of you.

To everyone who has crossed my path, positive and negative, I thank you for the lessons you have brought to my experience. My world is brighter because of you.

Finally, to my beautiful daughter, who 10 years ago changed my life forever. Thank you for the sunshine you pour into my soul. You are so special and will do incredible things. My buckets are constantly overflowing. I love you completely and unconditionally. You are my world.

Introduction

I have been a motivational speaker since the day I was born. If you gave me an audience, I would share with them anything I could to keep them informed and entertained. That has come in very handy over the last 12 years being in the health and wellness industry. I had the great pleasure of using that skill to convey my vast knowledge in a way people can easily understand and implement into their daily lives. At the end of most of my presentations, I end with the question, "What are you waiting for?" I've tried to drive home the point that most of us are truly just "waiting" to get what we want.

Look at the definition of "wait" from the Webster's dictionary:

> **Wait:** *To stay where one is or to delay action until a particular time or until something else happens.*

The key words in that definition are "stay" and "delay." Essentially, all of us are just staying where we are. We delay action on what we want. We put things off until the time feels perfect, which rarely happens, or until something forces us to make a change. Relationships can need attention and work. Communication can be a huge issue. If you wait, you're sure to end up in a failed relationship. We do the same thing with disease, for example, waiting until we have diabetes before we think about how much sugar and junk we eat. This cycle is dangerous.

We wait until we fail and then look for inspiration to make the changes we've been waiting for. We do a lot of waiting. And life is not waiting for you!

Over the last few years, I started thinking about things in my own life. What was I waiting for? I was in several relationships that served me negativity; I was unhappy in my career; and I felt challenges in being the best mother I could be. I saw myself incapable of getting anything I wanted. I was constantly moving further away from my goals and what I truly wanted to become and accomplish, yet life was not waiting. The years were passing by. Goals went unreached.

One day I decided I was sick and tired of the life I was leading. I was tired of sitting around and waiting for the right time or the right scenario to start accomplishing my desires. I started to research even further who and what was around me. I started reading powerful books from authors who had the same struggles as I. These people had seen real change in their lives. They had found the secret manual to life and I wanted it too, so I started a journey of learning. My clients and family had spent 14 years educating me on life, giving me their opinions on everything and essentially laying a foundation for my own learning. I began to study them and listen more. I paid attention to what they had to say and how they said it.

Through the Cleveland Clinic, I studied the brain, the body, our behaviors and how they all work together. I started reading and listening to even more positive and uplifting speakers like Wayne Dyer, Mike Murdoch, Neville Goddard and Louise Hay. I started to build my own spiritual relationship with prayer, meditation and living from my higher self. Kindness and thankfulness were easier to find by the day. All my learning came together in the pages of this book.

I have used my own techniques to change my entire life. I have found my true assignment here on Earth and am now able to move closer to it every day by following my passion and living in the highest vibration I can. By opening my awareness and learning all I can each day to better myself, I have stopped the waiting game. So I ask you….

Why. Wait? Awareness is Everything and your journey begins today!

Awareness
Is Everything

Thoughts and Feelings

Thought

We are incredibly complicated individuals. Our brains are much like intricate computer systems that house dozens more computer systems. All those networks interconnect to keep us going. In fact, if you started looking at all the mechanisms that keep our bodies functioning, you would quickly be overwhelmed. Though our bodies and brains are so very complicated, how and why we form bad behaviors is pretty simple.

Here's how we work: Thoughts lead to feelings, which lead to actions. That's it. It's as simple as that. Our thoughts lead to our feelings, which lead to all our actions. We can also look at it like this: What happens to us mentally festers inside emotionally and shows up physically. Every thought we have produces a feeling, which produces an action that we take. In order to change our thoughts, feelings and actions, we must first understand just how our systems work.

When looking at thought, I think of two quotes that I love. The first is:

If you think happy thoughts, you can fly.
— *Peter Pan*

Now, can we fly? Not really. But can we be free? Absolutely. And being free feels a lot like flying–the feeling of nothing holding us back or getting in the way, the freedom to move in whatever direction we choose. This is truly what we all seek; freedom to be who we are in a loving, accepting world. Our thoughts can provide us that freedom.

Peter Pan was the little boy who didn't want to grow up. He wanted to hold on to his youth and relish the joy, the laughter, the innocence and freedom that defines an ideal childhood. Think about kids. They don't care where they eat, what clothes they play in, whether they get their hands dirty or their clothes wet, where they live or what kind of car you drive. They just experience joy. Life is fun. A Popsicle stick and gum wrapper can provide hours of entertainment. Bubbles are exciting. Kids have a natural inclination towards thankfulness. They appreciate nature and new things. All of us started this way and this IS the way.

A huge part of the joy that children express comes from their ability to trust in things unseen. Children know how to believe. Whether it's in God, the Tooth Fairy, Santa Claus or the Easter Bunny; the point is… they believe. That blind faith gives them the freedom and ability to create magic in their imaginations. It is our adult world and its influence that breaks this quality in us all. Until children are influenced and changed, they know real joy. Even when they are neglected and hurt, they are apt to show unconditional love and adoration for that source.

The Bible says

> *Truly I tell you, anyone who will not receive the kingdom of God like a little child will never enter it.*
> — *Luke 18:17 (NIV)*

Your ability to embrace life with the faith and joy of a child will accelerate your blessings. The kingdom of God and endless blessings are awaiting you right now. Who knew that a character in a children's book would serve as a reminder of what gets us closer to blessings? Peter Pan was more than just a character; he was a great prophet of truth.

The second quote I love says this:

> *Change your thoughts, change your world.*
> — *Norman Vincent Peale*

Thoughts and Feelings

What we see and experience, and perceive as our world, is largely shaped by what we think. Our thoughts have a tremendous amount of power. When we change our perception of our current circumstances, our whole world changes before us. That is what I want this book to do for you. I want to help make your world better by showing you how to change your thoughts so you can change your world.

The Hamster Wheel

Psychologists have estimated that on average we have 60,000 thoughts per day. We think so much and our thoughts are so powerful that if we could harness all the energy from thoughts we could power a 25-watt light bulb. That says a lot for how strong our thoughts are. For most of us, our thinking is constant and encompasses a wide range of subjects, or we dwell on one subject or another. To change our thinking and make a true difference in our lives, first we must understand how thinking works.

Let's look at our conscious and subconscious minds. We already know that we actually only use a small percent of our brains or what we call the conscious mind. This is the area of our brains available for new thoughts and new learning. All our learning happens in the conscious mind.

The rest of our mind works on autopilot. This is the subconscious mind. It makes up the majority and accounts for almost all our daily functions.

Imagine the subconscious area of the brain like a giant hamster wheel that is constantly in motion. As we learn in our conscious minds, the information is gathered into this enormous hamster wheel, where it will turn forever. The more the same message is received, the stronger it turns the wheel.

Take basic math, for example. The first time you saw 2 + 2, you didn't know what that meant. The conscious mind learned the numbers and what they represented, and it became easier to understand and take on harder problems.

How about the first time you picked up a basketball? You didn't know how to dribble or shoot it into the net properly. As your coach taught you how to dribble and where to position your hands on the ball, your conscious mind gathered all that information and learned these new skills.

After a skill has been learned, this information takes a ride into the subconscious mind. I view it like a big playground slide. The information is gathered, placed at the top of the slide and then shoots down and empties into the hamster wheel, or subconscious mind. The hamster wheel will continue to spin that information for a long time. Until the message changes or new information is learned, the wheel will continue to turn and turn.

Look at your life now. If you haven't played basketball since college, could you go to a basketball court and play ball? Of course you could. Maybe not at your best, but you'd have a general feel for how to hold the ball, the position of your hands and body to dribble or shoot the ball. You may not be able to answer difficult math equations but do you have to think hard to add 2 + 2? Of course not. Your subconscious hamster wheel is still turning that information, so simple math comes naturally to you.

It's important to take a look at what you have been putting into that hamster wheel. When we were born, our minds were clean slates, blank canvases. We were born filled with love, joy and happiness. We had natural instincts and the innate ability to be abundantly thankful. Since that time, we have received messages from many sources, messages that conflict with the positive people we were born to be. What we learned about ourselves was learned from outside influences. Let's think about what we might have experienced during childhood.

Maybe you grew up in a home like my friend Mary's. Her dad was absent because he had to work all the time. When he was home, he barely spoke and when he did, he said things like "Sit down," "Shut up" or "Get out of the way." She doesn't have a flood of happy memories from time spent with him. He never attended special events, with the exception of one high school softball season. (No games, no piano recitals, no programs at school or chorus concerts.) Before her parents divorced when she turned 12, she barely knew her dad existed. Between his full-time job and the side businesses her family owned and operated, she really doesn't remember receiving any attention from him. He was just a man who ate, sat and slept in her home. The moments she remembers all have to do with discipline, not fun times.

My experience growing up was very similar to Mary's. My dad provided so well for our family. He worked all day long and then came home at night and spent hours tending to our farm. I only have a few memories with my dad, most of them from our farm. I can vividly recall the day when he taught me to ride a bike. Like most children, there was one thing I wanted more than anything: my daddy's attention. I had no shortage of love for him or the desire for a relationship with him, despite the reality of our situation. Wanting his attention all those years and not receiving it sent such direct messages to my hamster wheel as "Daddy doesn't care," and "You're not good enough." By the time I reached high school, I gave up on finding that love from him and went searching for it in all the wrong places instead. Most of us can relate to this concept, no matter how we were raised. As we grow, we receive lots of information about ourselves — both positive and negative — all of which has an impact on what we believe about ourselves.

My father loves me to the end of the world and back, but that didn't change my interpretation of the messages I received from my perception of my world growing up. My father did what he had to do for our family to survive. He provided for us in countless ways. These are things we can't see as a child. We see them looking back and by that time our perceptions have already formed our thoughts about ourselves and our reality.

If one or both of your parents were absent when you were a child, that sent many messages to you about who you are, how valuable you are and how you rank in life and society. So many people are starving for attention, desperately wanting to feel seen, loved, valued. Some of you might have had parents who were much the opposite. Maybe they showed you too much attention and were overbearing, not allowing you to establish the skills to think and act for yourself. Many of you were raised with a feeling of never having enough. That feeling led to all sorts of negative views of yourself. Some of you have turned to addictions to fill that void.

Our influences feed our learning and conscious minds and eventually all those messages end up in the hamster wheel. You learn a lot of negative things about yourself and about your reality from immediate family, friends, spouses, children, workplaces, churches and the media. There are messages sent to you from all directions. They are reinforced daily by the influences that are around you now. What you believe to be true about who you are and the values you hold is being backed up every day by the hamster wheel. The wheel will keep turning that information until you change what you're feeding it. Change starts with awareness.

So take a look at what's in your wheel. What thoughts are moving around in your mind? What relationships have you had? What impressions have been put there that may not be true about you? Were you always told you couldn't do something? Is that really true? Or have you just put it in the wheel and assumed its truth?

Your mind is like a highway. Up until this point you have made no effort to manage the traffic on that highway, so it has become blocked and cha-otic. There is no room left for anything positive. You allow others in your present life and ideas from your past determine what gets to stay and jam up the highway. Each vehicle on your road is a thought. Most of them are negative and lead to worry and reliving the past. Your mind fills with doubt and fear and many unwanted emotions. This thought highway is dangerous for everyone. Clear the road and carefully choose the cars you allow back on.

What You Hear When You Listen

Not long ago I was meditating and praying over my book. I needed instruction on what to do next and what my next step should be. In my quiet time, the following scripture came to me:

> *Blessed are those who find wisdom, those who gain understanding, for she is more profitable than silver and yields better returns than gold. She is more precious than rubies; nothing you desire can compare with her. Long life is in her right hand; in her left hand are riches and honor. Her ways are pleasant ways, and all her paths are peace. She is a tree of life to those who take hold of her; those who hold her fast will be blessed.*
> — *Proverbs 3:13-22 (NIV)*

So I started my quest for wisdom. I wanted more wisdom on what to do and say. Wisdom is a giant key to all the successes we are looking for, as it helps us determine which doors to open and which to close. In the Bible, many who prayed to obtain more were divinely blessed. It seems to me that it would be smart for all of us to search for more wisdom.

I spent a week focusing on obtaining more wisdom for this book. Each time I sat quietly, a voice inside seemed to shout, "Just shut up." As a motivational teacher and coach, I do a lot of talking. The thought of me shutting up seemed crazy. Everything I do requires heavy communication, but the instruction stayed very clear: "Just shut up." After two days of clear messages, I made plans to spend an entire day in silence.

That Tuesday morning, I got up and headed to work as I normally do. On this particular day, I was teaching 2 Zumba classes and leading a weight loss support group, and I did it all in silence. It was amazing to me that teaching in silence was the easy part. Actually hearing what was going on around me was much more of a struggle.

The dozens of women I worked with that morning had terrible thought highways. Each of them were filled with mantras of failure and lack. So many expressed fear and lack of confidence to achieve many of their goals. If one was talking about something negative, the whole tribe chimed in and added to the discouragement. Very few offered up kind words or optimism about their struggles. What amazed me the most was that before I spent a day listening, I had never truly heard just how negative everyone else was. I was so busy talking to others that it escaped my notice that these women, some of whom are the most faithful women I know, had no faith in themselves. I was shocked by what I heard. I couldn't imagine the monstrous traffic jams on their thought highway that were causing this negative internal language.

One woman came up and asked me what I was doing. I wrote on a piece of paper that I had prayed for wisdom and the answer I received was that if I were quiet for a full day, I'd get answers. She looked right at me and said, "That'll never work! You're absolutely crazy!" This is how we talk and communicate with each other. This expression came from a woman I love dearly. She's a wonderful woman who I know in my heart loves me very much, believes in me and my program and frankly feels like family to me. But when it comes to transferring negative energy to each other, we do it a lot, naturally. When we consider what we do to relative strangers, imagine the damage we do to the people closest in our lives. In that moment it all clicked. This is what I was supposed to witness and the message that I was to drive home. Your thought highway is powerful.

Not only does it damage you, but it wreaks havoc on others. All that negative energy just adds pollution to our thought highways.

Power In Your Words

ll through my day of silence, I heard various versions of the same thing — negative affirmations that feed people's hamster wheels all day long. "I am not," "I cannot," "I will not," "I should not," "I could not," "I don't know how," "It's not enough," "I can't do that," and the list goes on. It was amazing to me how so many faithful women who believe in God and His divine grace spent a lot of time putting limitations on what He could do. All instead of asking for their desires and believing He had the power to make it happen.

It says in the Bible:

And God said unto Moses, I am that I am. And he said, Thus shalt you say unto the children of Israel, I AM hath sent me unto you.
                        — Exodus 3:14 (KJV)

This is a powerful verse for us to learn and apply to our lives for this is where we learn God's name.

"I am." I remember the first time I read this in one of my favorite Wayne Dyer books, *Wishes Fulfilled*. I fully understood the power of this passage. It has changed my life ever since. I AM is God's name, so I'm much more careful about how I use it. It is crucial to be careful of how you use it too.

Don't let your strongest words, God's name, represent negative things. Of all the curse words you are conscious not to say, these should go on the top of the list. You are loved, valued, beautiful, talented, awesome, amazing, forgiven, capable of anything and successful. You are all these things and more. Don't let your internal language say, "I am not," "I can't," or "I won't." It is defeating to put limits on yourself or on God. This kind of thinking does not belong in your hamster wheel. Thoughts lead to feelings and those feelings lead to actions. Begin changing your actions by starting with your thoughts and your internal conversation with yourself.

Feelings

et's take a look at our emotions, or feelings, and how they work with thought. We experience many emotions — some good, some bad and some neutral. But all emotions have the potential to be very powerful. Besides the power of our thoughts themselves, we have an internal accelerator, which can strengthen the power of our thoughts in a positive or a negative way.

A thought is similar to a flame. Having a thought is like striking a match or lighter. Imagine this: "I had a bad day." Thinking it gives power to spark the flame. But at this point that single flame is small; it's weak. Ever sprayed a lighter with hair spray? The small flame in the lighter ignites into a raging flame that can shoot as far as a few feet. It can be quite scary if you are not anticipating it. The hair spray is an instant accelerator of the flame. The flame is now significantly more powerful.

One day, as a teen, my dad brought home a 1956 Chevy truck to rebuild. This was dad's project and took up a lot of his time, but is a great memory for me nonetheless. We had it fixed up and painted bright red with yellow flames. My dad drove it at a local drag racing venue. That truck was amazing. I remember how excited I felt every time we got in it. At 15 mph, the truck would start bouncing. At 25 mph, we were bouncing even harder and I couldn't keep from giggling. By the time we reached 40, my head almost touched the ceiling and that nauseated feeling would set in. Just when I thought I couldn't take another moment of the ride, my daddy would push the button on the nitrous tank and that truck would accelerate to 60 mph in a matter of seconds. The nitrous tank was an accelerator for the gas in the truck. It pushed it faster and made it more focused and powerful. It's the same with how we think and feel.

The more feeling we put into any thought, the faster and more dramatic our actions will be.

Controlling Emotion

One of the things we can do to help our thoughts is to change the conversations we have with ourselves. This is called self-talk. Most of us have a very negative chatterbox in our minds. This is much more than a conversation or the "I am's" we have talked about already. It is an internal language that we have learned and practiced for many years of our lives. Many of us have been beating ourselves up with messages others have imposed on us. We must change the conversation. As long as we engage in negative self-talk, we continue to have negative feelings, which lead to negative actions.

The thought highway should be like an open road and we should carefully choose the thoughts we put on it. In my life, my mother has more influence over my thoughts than anyone else. Her opinions mean more to me than anyone's. I want her to be proud of me, to support my ideas and choices. Because I value her feedback so much, she can make an innocent comment that sends my thoughts in all the wrong directions. Those thoughts are joined by an eruption of feelings and her warnings or suggestions leave my mind spinning. Sometimes her warnings or suggestions leave my mind caught up in the thought. I've had to learn to decide which thoughts I allow on my highway. I've had to practice only receiving messages that make me feel good. I've had to learn to choose what I allow to stay in my thought highway and let the rest pass by. It's about receiving the positive pieces of the message and letting go of the negative ones. When you do this positive feelings will show up to support your thoughts.

Some people in our lives are like rest stops on the thought highway. You intended to stop for a just a moment to use the bathroom but by the time you are back in your car, you bought a hot dog, made a phone call, filled up on gas and spent 20 minutes there. Avoid all the rest stops. Realize you are filled from within with everything you need. Keep moving and keep the traffic clear.

Choose what happens in your mind, what information is allowed to come in and become part of the hamster wheel. When people say things that I choose not to let onto my thought highway, I put up a "ROAD BLOCK" sign and prevent that information from finding a place on my road. I know what I believe about who I am and what I can be. Though I respect and love all those around me, I define myself.

We all define ourselves. Our thoughts, not choices, will determine how we feel and how we will then behave.

Attitude

The only difference between a good day and a bad day is your attitude.

— *Dennis Brown*

I love this quote because it represents the first action step in changing thoughts and feelings. Attitude is major and we live in a world that has downright nasty and rotten attitudes. We are surrounded every day by others who are drowning in their negative spirits. Anger, hurt, depression, sadness, betrayal and unhappiness consume so many of us. We can find it everywhere we go. When we get caught up with negative people and negative circumstances, it's hard to maintain a positive attitude. Once negative thoughts set in, negative feelings and actions will follow.

When I was still a new mom to my daughter, I was divinely blessed in my business. That year everyone who worked for us received a bonus to brag about. I spent every penny of mine on a brand-new house. A big, beautiful, 4-bedroom, 2-story property in a development people yearned to live in.

One year later I was ready to remodel. I decided one weekend that I wanted to paint the upstairs of my incredible home. I made a detailed plan and headed to Lowe's, where I purchased paint and supplies—light pink for my daughter's room, dark grey for the middle living room and a medium tan color for my bedroom.

I started painting as soon as I got home. I made a place for my daughter, who was 3 at the time, to play in the middle living room and began working on her pink bedroom. Because the room was empty, I worked very fast and she played very well in the other room. She didn't come into the bedroom once to see what I was doing. She listened to me like a good girl, playing with her toys and listening to her music.

As I was finishing the pink room I noticed an area of the wall where paint was streaming down onto the white baseboard. Being the perfectionist I am, I had to get something to wipe it clean and headed to the door of the bedroom. I stopped at the door and thought a few moments.

To get to the bathroom and the only handy tissues or towels, I had to travel 10 feet away from the pink room. My daughter was playing nicely in the same spot and waved to me as I stood there. All I had to do was get toilet paper or a towel and return to the room. It would take about 30 seconds. What could happen in 30 seconds?

I left the pink room and headed for the bathroom. Within a few seconds, I had rolled some toilet paper onto my hand. When I had a fair amount I tore it off and headed back to her room. As I crossed through the door, my mouth dropped. She had come in, picked up my almost full bucket of paint and dumped it over her head. She was spinning in a circle, screaming, "Whee! Whee! Whee!" I gasped as the tears started to stream down my face. Not only was pink paint dripping from every orifice of my child, it was now sprayed all over every inch of the brand-new carpet. She had poured at least a half-gallon over her head.

I'm not sure now if it was seconds or minutes, but when the shock wore off, I scooped her up and ran into the bathroom. She had long, gorgeous brown curls and I was having a terrible time getting the paint out of them. The paint was even dripping from her eyelashes.

I truly didn't know what to do. Nothing—not my mother, my parenting classes, books I'd read, upbringing I'd experienced — nothing had prepared me for this. I was sobbing and screaming at the same time, mad as hell at this little girl. I was giving it to her, telling her how bad she was for picking up the paint and what a mess she had caused.

By the time I had her mostly clean and dried off, I was able to assess the room. There was pink paint everywhere. Her new carpet was ruined. The carpet to the bathroom had sprinkles of paint. Pink paint splattered the windows and the door frame, and covered the bathroom and tub. I put her to bed and called my mom. I was a mess. My brand-new house was ruined. I was very disheartened.

After some reflection, I decided that I had learned a valuable lesson: Paint while children are sleeping. So I headed back upstairs to tackle as much of the grey room as I could while she was asleep. By midnight I had almost finished and was ecstatic to end my day on such a positive note. I put the paint cans away and washed out all the brushes. I left only the roller pan, almost empty, and the roller on the floor beside some furniture, almost out of sight. I went to bed tired, but happy.

At 3:00 a.m. I was awakened to the sensation of a wet paint roller crossing my face and very excited giggles. When I opened my eyes I saw my daughter. All the lights were on and she was running the roller down the side of my bed and up my face. Again, I'm not sure if it was seconds or minutes, but when the shock wore off I jumped up, grabbed the roller from her hand and started to cry. I knew right away by the lights shining throughout the upstairs that my face and bed were not the only things covered in lovely dark grey paint. As the tears continued to stream, I yelled at her for getting out of bed and being a bad girl. I walked into the living area where the paint tray had been and gasped. She had used the roller to paint several areas of the floor, my bookcase, and my books. The carpet for the entire room was ruined. I continued to cry and berate her for being bad. I took her into bed with me and we cried ourselves to sleep.

When I opened my eyes, I realized I hadn't been dreaming. There was still paint on my hands and I could feel the dried paint on the sheets. I was so defeated. The thought of the ruined carpet in my lovely home made me cringe every time it crossed my mind. An overwhelming feeling of loss was within me and I continued to take it out on my daughter with my mouth.

After breakfast I decided I had to finish what I started and paint my bedroom. I had spent the money on the paint, had taken the time off to do it and had already learned some valuable lessons. The central lesson seemed to be not leaving the paint on the floor where my child could get her hands on it. I put some thought into it and decided I'd take a couple of kitchen bar stools up to my bedroom. That seemed like the best way to keep the paint off the floor.

I put her in the same area in the living room and put up some small barriers to keep her where she belonged, then set up the paint in my bedroom. The gallon of tan paint went on one bar stool and the supplies went on the other. I climbed the ladder and started painting. A few brush strokes in, I heard her calling, "Mommy!" and I quickly realized she sounded closer than she should be. As I came down the ladder to see what was going on, she barreled into the room. Running towards me with her arms open wide, screaming, "Mommy!", she pushed over the bar stool with the paint can. The entire gallon of paint sprayed through the air and landed in a huge glob in the middle of my room. I can still see myself moving in slow motion and hear the sound of my voice screaming, "No!!!" as the paint went flying. I can still see how mortified she was. I didn't have to tell her she was a bad girl at this point. She knew it and was already crying before I got to her. At that point, all I could do was cry too. I was completely defeated and so was she.

This story is a favorite in my collection. If you are an experienced parent now or have spent any time with kids, you know what a challenge it is to learn the do's and dont's of raising a child. We all make mistakes that become great lessons. My mistakes in this story are bigger than just trying to paint near a 3-year old. These lessons run much deeper.

Now, almost 8 years later, I have no attachment to that house. It was just a box I was blessed to live in for a few years. A box that was made of wood and provided shelter and access to electricity and water. But looking back, I see now that my daughter is my meaning. She has value. She is more than a box that provides shelter and electricity and water; she is a source of inspiration. She is beauty manifested as each of us can be. During that time in my life, I was caught up in the wrong kind of happiness and my attitude showed it. Based on everything I've learned and what I've used to enhance my own life, I would have handled this much differently now. Awareness would change everything.

When I walked in the room and caught her with the paint all over, spinning in a circle, I'd still have scooped her up and headed to the bathroom, but I would have had on my best smile. I would have washed her up, but I would have relished it and been sure to take her picture. I would have instructed her on her mistake, but I would have held my tone and used words to empower her, not teach her she has less value. She didn't see a mess or ruined carpet; she saw joy.

When the roller went across my face at 3:00 a.m. and I opened my eyes to her howling laughter at what she had done, I'd have laughed too, not scowled at her in anger and frustration. I am the adult that left the roller on the floor. And finally, when she ran to me, excited to be free from the cage I'd built, arms open, calling my name, wanting only my love, I'd have embraced her wholeheartedly and counted that blessing among my highest. Like Peter Pan, she was just thinking happy thoughts and yearning for that joy, that freedom.

Friends, it is in our attitudes that we gain freedom. Attitude impacts thought. Imagine right now that you have a flat tire on the way to work. You are already running 10 minutes late. So you sit in your car and start thinking. You think about being late, the inconvenience of the flat and how much it will cost you. Your thoughts lead to feelings and those feelings intensify your thoughts. Before you know it, you've had a terrible experience. It takes a horribly long time to fix your flat, as you anticipated. Your workday is dramatically affected by your negative attitude. Your personal life suffers and you are exhausted.

If I was stuck on a highway with a flat tire I couldn't change, as a single woman there are only 3 things I'd be thinking. One: All things happen for a reason. So thank you, God, for the reason I am in this spot. Two: I hope the tow truck driver owns the company and is really cute. Three: I hope he's single too! That's about it! I have learned to take each negative opportunity and find some reason for thankfulness in it. Not all negatives are negative. So many times our lowest moments are when the greatest miracles can come. I love this quote:

> *We turn to God for help when our*
> *foundations are shaking, only to learn that it is*
> *God who is shaking them.*
> — *Charles C. West*

This quote helps put our attitudes into perspective. Sometimes the road we travel doesn't make sense to us. It's important to stay focused on where we're going and travel with great anticipation of all things divine. You never know what divine appointment is being set up for you. Show up ready to receive!! Garth Brooks also says it well:

Some of God's greatest gifts are unanswered prayers.
— *Garth Brooks*

How many times did you not receive what you wanted, but can count that as a blessing now? The job you thought you wanted, the relationship you thought was best–there are dozens of requests in our lives that are better left unfulfilled.

Having a positive attitude comes down to how we embrace each opportunity and moment we are given. It can be very contagious to those around us, but it takes some practice. We have to realize when we start that the people around us will not understand at first. They will be confused as to who we have become and why we no longer match the level where they operate.

When mom and I moved to Pennsylvania from Virginia to open our first business, we hugged everybody. Where I come from, hugging is as common as "hello." You always follow both a hello and a goodbye with a big ole hug. I'll never forget signing up my first client and seeing the look on her face when we put our arms out for a hug. She looked at us like we were crazy. She was hesitant and taken aback. When she hugged us, she tried hard not to squeeze us or make too much body contact. That went on with hundreds of women we met in our first year of business. It's been 14 years now and every time we see that first client, she comes to us with open arms to embrace us. She wants to express that love and she hugs tightly, too. Our loving attitudes became contagious and now our clients always find excuses to give us or another client a hug. Some women won't leave without hugging the employee on staff that day. It feels good, and deep down, feeling good is what we all want.

Having a good attitude and expressing positive energy felt a little easier where I grew up. Everybody knew everybody. You could walk through Wal-Mart and know everyone around you without even seeing their faces. People waved to each other on the street. When I moved away to bigger places and waved at my neighbor for the first time, they looked at me as if to say, "Who are you and what do you want?" Be a waver. Let people wonder. After a few months here, everyone in my development knew I was going to wave and you know what? A lot of them started to wave back. Let your good attitude be contagious.

Thankfulness

*He is a wise man that does not grieve for
the things he has not but rejoices for those which
he has.*

— *Epitas*

his is another of my favorite quotes. If we
want to fix what is broken in our thought
processes, the best place to start is with thankfulness. Every single one of us has something to be
thankful for. I'm sure we could come up with a
list of what's wrong: "I'm not financially where I
want to be. I'm not where I want to be in my life.
My relationships are not working out right. I don't
have the job I want. Things at work and in life are
not so good."

Despite the lists we could make of things that
are wrong, there is a longer list of blessings we have
received and are still receiving. Most of us have 10
fingers and 10 toes. Most of us are able to walk and
our breathing is normal and healthy. We can talk and
use our hands and hold down a job. We probably
have people in our lives who love us. We can see and

hear and feel. All those things mean our lives are a lot better than those of many other people in this world. We have the greatest gift of all–the gift of choosing how our emotions will respond to our thoughts.

Thankfulness is where we can truly start the process of changing how we think. It's not so easy for us to sit down and say, "I am beautiful. I am successful. I am loved. I am confident. I am worthy. I feel good. I am well." That's especially hard when the reality around us doesn't support that idea. Take the thought, "I have everything I need. I am prosperity." If we are in a season of financial hardship, that phrase is exactly what we should use. Even though that phrase doesn't match what the hamster wheel has been taught and everything about us rejects that idea, we need to use that phrase anyway.

Thankfulness is the way to get past our inability to believe in a divine thought such as, "I have everything I need. I am prosperity." Instead, begin with something easier to convince yourself about. In this example, that is being thankful for the money we have. Instead of looking at what is not on the table, start looking at what is. For example, if you want beans and rice but only have beans, get thankful for the beans, rather than focusing on not having the rice. God doesn't want to hear that. He wants to hear us embrace what He has given us so He can give us more. He wants to know we want more and He wants to see how thankful and in awe we are to have it. Through thankfulness and gratitude, more blessings come pouring down. The more we celebrate our thankfulness, the better. It works so well with helping to change our attitudes as well.

Thankfulness isn't just good for keeping our thoughts focused on positive things. It is also really good for our accelerators, our emotions. Here's an example:

Think of someone you love and are thankful for, maybe a spouse, a child or a parent. Really imagine and feel how thankful you are for them. Do you feel the warmth that creates? The rush you feel inside may even bring you to tears. That's the most beautiful thing. Think thankful thoughts and you will feel good inside. It will help your actions stay positive as well and that circle of positivity will rain blessings over you. ***Why. Wait.*** Positive things want to show up in our life. Those hamster wheels want to run on positive energy. Attitude and thankfulness are two of the most powerful players when it comes to changing thought and feelings and having better actions. They work hand in hand to help us change and we need them both. Let me tell you, it's hard at first, but it gets easier with practice.

Learn To Make Positive Movies

We need to start creating dreams that feel good. When I talk about dreams, I'm not just talking about the ones you have when you sleep. I mean the ones that play in your head all the time. We play different films in our minds every day. We create movies fueled with emotion that harvest major actions and reactions. It's a good example of how thoughts and feelings work best together.

Look at this scenario. Your daughter, who lives several states away, has 2 children and is in a rocky marriage. Her job is not secure and you worry about her being laid off. The two of you only speak on the phone on Thursdays after 5 p.m. when she is home from work and settled. On a random Tuesday, your daughter calls you at 3 p.m. You miss the call and she doesn't leave a message. You immediately think to yourself how odd it is that she would be calling you in the afternoon like this. You add to that thought that something *must* be wrong. You then start to worry about what could be wrong. The kids? Her husband?

Did she lose her job? Did the house burn down? Within a few short moments, you have added anxiety and fear and played out several negative short movies in your head. Your negative thoughts lead to feelings of worry and they will show up in your actions. Your body requires you to do something to reduce the stress you feel. An action will show up. Maybe you call every phone number you have for her over and over. Maybe you hit the kitchen for food to calm your nerves. Maybe you smoke. Maybe you get so panicked you call your son-in-law or call your daughter's workplace. How stupid we feel after an episode like this when she calls back to ask for an ingredient in a recipe or for the birth date of her grandma. We are all so apt to create a negative scenario before acquiring enough information to really know if this is true, and we play these short movies in our minds all day long. Some will be positive, but most will be negative. We jump to the negative conclusion almost instinctively, without thinking about it.

I've seen the example above play out in real life. My mother used to be quite the worrier. If she couldn't reach me on the phone when she thought I should have answered, she would drive to my house to check on me. She could create a high level of panic in a few short hours. Other mothers I know have children living hours away. They can't get in the car to go check on them. Instead they will snack or indulge in sweet treats or a glass of wine that give temporary relief. No matter what, the thought will lead to a feeling and an action.

A friend of mine went through this scenario. His mom started to think negative thoughts regarding her son's finances. She quickly became overwhelmed with worry and fear that something was going to go wrong that would leave her son and his family in trouble. She eventually used his password, given to her in confidence in case of an emergency, to look into her son's checking account. Seeing the information made his mother worry even more. She began to analyze all his spending and felt that he was not making good choices for himself or his family. The mother grew so concerned over his spending habits that she sat down with him and his wife and gave them a stern lecture on saving money.

The son and his wife were stunned. The son said, "We opened a new checking account months ago and we have more than enough money. That is an account we use for things we want and enjoy. We are doing fine and I'm extremely hurt you would violate my trust instead of speaking to me about it. Checking my account when I am 37 years old is way out of line." Thoughts led to feelings which led to actions. My friend's mother couldn't help herself. She was so worried and so worked up she had to find relief. She had to see for herself and then act on what she saw. Instead, she needed to fix her thoughts and feelings. My friend didn't speak to his mother for a few days and it took years to rebuild the trust in their relationship.

Creating dreams from worry is never good and the outcome is most often negative. I've been in several relationships where trust was broken. Many times my partner would not answer the phone or respond to me in what I thought was an appropriate amount of time. Immediately my head would begin to spin with thoughts of betrayal and distrust. I would automatically assume he was lying and use old information to back up those thoughts and feelings. My thoughts would fester until he got back to me and then I would make serious accusations, all based on old patterns of thoughts and feelings. Sometimes I was right, but many times I wasn't. My reactions didn't change, because my thoughts were so vivid and my emotions so strong that I couldn't control my behavior. I would have the accusations out of my mouth before I could think.

Stay ahead of your thoughts and feelings by playing movies in your mind that feel good. When you catch yourself watching a scene in the negative, rewrite the script! We can't always be watching scary thrillers, horror movies or dramas in our heads. Look for the light-hearted, feel-good movies that project the idea of what you want!

Get Generous

In order to change the scenarios that are playing out in our imaginations, we can't just
become better thinkers. We must become better
feelers of positive feelings. That may sound easy.
Yes, we are great feelers, but the negative is where
we do most of our feeling and it doesn't serve us.
We're good at being angry, sad, depressed, discour-
aged, unhappy and all things negative. These negative feelings come so easily because all of us are so
absorbed in them. We throw them around to each
other all the time. It's easy to encounter negative
feelings anywhere we go. People are oozing them.
We have to learn to start practicing the opposite.

My clients often express how hard it is to feel
positive. Many of them don't know where to find
joy any more except through their addictions and
negative behaviors. I hear things like, "I don't know
how to feel good when all the things in my life seem
to be crashing. I don't know how to stay up when
this situation that's happening in my life wants to
push me down. I am not able to manage what I
have and generate anything positive. I am numb
and have no feeling at all. I don't know how to get

to the place of feeling something better. My job is negative, my spouse is negative. I'm surrounded."

Until we can get to a place where positive feelings such as joy, happiness, love, excitement and elation come to us freely, we have to use tools to create positive emotions. Maintaining a positive attitude and being thankful are the first steps in that process. To accelerate our efforts and create feelings to match, get generous.

I'm not talking about spending a lot of money. In fact, I'm not talking about spending any money at all. I'm talking about what we can do with the power within us to create a power within us. By being someone who goes out of their way to lift others with our words and our actions, we will create a feeling of joy that is untouchable and addictive. It will create a feeling that far surpasses any negative addictions we have established.

I am now one of those people. In the last few years I have worked very hard in this particular area. I am generous with my words and I do my best to use them for good whenever the opportunity arrives. I listen for little messages that let me know when there are good opportunities. I'm not perfect, but I go out of my way to lift others up. If someone walks by and I like their haircut, I tell them. I am the person who randomly walks up to anyone and gives them a compliment I think they deserve. I am the woman who stops other women to complement their smell. I am the woman who stops someone in the grocery store to tell them how nice they look. I am the woman who will call a service line to give a compliment about a great employee or an exceptional experience. I go out of my way to spread good to others. I try to take actions that are of help to everyone. I've pulled over on the side of the road to remove a hubcap or garbage can from the street. I've taken shopping carts blowing in the parking lot and returned them where they belonged. I'm every lemonade stand's dream.

It's who I am and it's awesome. It feels so good to have someone look at you in utter shock and say, "Do you know how good that feels? I haven't had someone tell me something nice in ages. You have made my day." Or to see the look on someone's face when you say, "Go ahead in front of me. I'm not in a hurry." They get a buzz, but I get a way bigger buzz giving the blessing than they do receiving it. When it comes to changing attitude, thankfulness is the best place to start. Your mouth has power and the more you use it to lift others up, the more you will be lifted too.

Actually seeing the positive in others and passing that message to them through the generosity of our words and actions can be difficult. We have received so many messages about judging others. We have been taught that physical beauty sets us apart from one another and defines our value. Many of us have such low self-esteem that anyone we think looks better than we perceive ourselves to look is thrown into a category and judged in our mind. This low self-esteem has been forced on us by dozens of influences and the hamster wheel continues to produce that information. This is an example of something I went through when I was in my unhealthy mind and body, when my thoughts, feelings and actions were dominated by the negative. It sounded something like this...

Imagine you are going to a party with a group that you are not comfortable or familiar with. You will likely feel out of place where you are going. You consider yourself to be a little overweight and you need to have your hair done in a bad way. You have kids and a full schedule, so you don't have the time to care for yourself as you would like. The outfit you are wearing, the feelings you have about yourself and the anxiety you feel about going already have you uncomfortable before you even arrive.

When you do arrive, you feel underdressed and out of place. The thoughts of how you look lead to negative feelings about yourself. A stunning woman enters the room and has the attention of everyone, including your spouse. She works the room in a stunning red dress you'd need to lose some pounds to fit into. She has gorgeous breasts that sit up perfectly where they belong and are on display for everyone to see. Her blonde locks don't even look real and you're sure she has a private make-up artist. Her jewelry is expensive and her heels are only a pipe dream for your closet anymore. This woman is so sexy and confident that even her ears are a turn-on.

You're already feeling insecure. Thoughts of what your spouse is thinking combined with your thoughts about yourself quickly overwhelm you. I mean, you've had kids! You have battle wounds under your clothes. The thoughts and feelings pour in. Inadequacy takes the lead and your heart is racing. You're not sure what to do to calm down. You want to burst into tears or tell someone off. The lady in the red dress approaches you and your husband. As she talks to you it becomes quite clear that she is not the dumb blonde, boob job woman you had her pegged to be. She raised 3 amazing children, can hold a great conversation and is very successful. You notice how your husband can't help but be enthralled by her aura, as you are too. She is not only stunning on the outside but on the inside. She is so many things you want to be.

As you do more thinking and feeling, you become even more insecure. That insecurity mixes with shame for what you initially felt about her and anger at what you feel toward your husband. The mixture of thoughts and feelings is too much to handle. You must act to stop this level of stress and anxiety. You will reach to what has helped you in the past.

The tornado you created picks up so much speed you just want the thoughts and feelings to change. You have a glass of wine, then two, then three, then too much. You say something stupid. You trip and embarrass yourself and your partner. You get in the car and can't shut up. You lay into your husband with all your insecurities by spouting accusations about what he was thinking and feeling. You continue on and insult the woman in the red dress to make yourself feel better. "I'm sure she just had a boob job anyway. No woman with kids has boobs like that." "I'd look that way too with all that money." Before you know it, you are spouting negativity everywhere. Your thoughts led your feelings so strongly that you acted within a short time frame with negative behaviors.

Changing your thoughts and feelings would change your reaction and your feelings about the lady in the red dress. We need to turn negative thinking about others around. When I started this journey, I was just like most of us. My head was filled with judgment all the time. I didn't go out of my way to get to know other people. It's not easy to express good news to others all the time. If I had a positive thought about someone else, I never would have projected that thought onto them. I would have used it to feed my own insecurities and judge that person, just like the scenario above. Prior to changing my thinking with my attitude and thankfulness, I would always turn what I saw as beauty into something I could judge based on something I felt I was lacking. I learned to change my emotions about feeling "less than" by changing my thoughts. The change in my thoughts led to healthier feelings of appreciation and prevented my judging actions. When I see something beautiful or outstanding to me, I actually see it, feel appreciation for it and share it. That sharing creates the kind of euphoria that can replace the need to feel negative and judge, creating joy within and around us.

There have been a few times in my life when I was in the kind of darkness where nothing brought me joy. I have battled strong depression for most of my life. There was a short time when my daughter was little that even she could barely stimulate my feelings. I was so numb and in so much darkness that I couldn't see an ounce of light.

To bring light into my darkness, I had to be the light. God works within each of us to lift us out of the dark. I saw no one to lift me out, no one to help me see the way or give me the will to fight, even my child, until God stirred within me that through Him, my attitude, my thankfulness and my generosity, I could have all things. When I decided to be the light, the light grew and it replaced my darkness.

Remember, this is not based on what we can buy for someone else. It's about words and actions. Be nice to people who cut us off while driving.

Remember to say "please" and "thank you" to everyone who provides a service to us. Help the short lady get the item from the top shelf at the grocery store. Be patient when there is a line and let someone else go first. BE the light. When we are in a place where we can't find positive feelings anywhere else, we need to turn to that generosity.

The Teenager Mentality

It takes courage to grow up and become who you really are.

— *e. e. cummings*

This is a great quote for all of us. I'm not saying by any means that we are not grown up. Many of us have been physically grown up for a good while now. I'm talking about our spiritual selves.

Have you ever raised a teenager? Even if you haven't, I'm sure you understand that it's a challenging, demanding experience for all involved. Teenagers don't listen to anyone and know everything. They procrastinate and can be needy, demanding, ungrateful and disrespectful. They want to do things their way and often do, which leads to dramatic disasters and cries of, "I told you so!" from their parents. Teenagers can be an absolute struggle. You just want to shake them sometimes and say, "Knock it off! Your way is not the way!!"

We often act like those very teenagers towards God. Our God is a giving God. He wants to hand the blessings out and it's clear that our attitudes and degree of thankfulness matters significantly. But what do we do instead? We ask Him to guide us and direct us and love us and forgive us and give to us and watch over us... The list goes on and on. And then we do our own thing, ignore direction, do not follow the call, hurt others, hold forgiveness from others, lack thankfulness for what He has already given us and then ask for more and more. What we have to do is quite simple: Grow up in our spiritual selves.

The grown-up version of our spiritual selves isn't the teenagers we are now. We need to become listeners of direction and instruction. Be grateful for everything we have and express that openly and constantly. Be positive and look forward to blessings. Be faithful, with our eyes on the destination and no worries about the journey. Expect all things in divine order. Operate through unconditional love and a giving spirit. Lift others up and go out of our way to do well. Do our best to be like Jesus in the way He was with people. Stay focused on all positive energy. No matter what others have been through, what they have done or how bad they have been, love them. It is time to grow up into the spiritual adults we are meant to be.

Like a Great Oak

Who and what are around you will either feed your strengths or your weaknesses.
— Mike Murdoch

This quote is from one of my favorite teachers, Dr. Mike Murdoch. I have read many of his books and enjoyed many of his presentations on my spiritual journey. He helped me get started on my own road to discovery. This particular quote has changed my life. Many years ago it became my mantra and I had an amazing adventure searching out the power of my influences. I studied in my business among my clients and in my personal life, which was the most eye opening. Last year I earned a certificate with the Cleveland Clinic, specializing in the effects of these influences and the roles they play in nutrition, activity and associated behaviors. At this point I could write a whole book on that subject alone. What Mike Murdoch opened up in

my mind many years ago has turned into knowledge of others and myself that I would never trade.
My eyes have been opened too wide.

Who and what feeds us, our thoughts, and the
hamster wheel has a huge impact on who we are
and how we behave. The company we keep has
some of the greatest impact on us. My grandma
often used to say, "When you lay with the pigs, you
always come out smelling like them."

Imagine your spirit, your attitude and positive
image of yourself and the world as an oak tree. When
you were born, your oak tree was an enormous
structure. The roots of your oak tree ran deep and
strong. It was also extremely tall and wide, extending
far into the heavens. That oak tree has been broken
down branch by branch since you were born and
there are still influences in your life whittling away at
your tree. As a child you couldn't control these influences, but now you have the power to decide what
influences affect your oak tree.

Woodpeckers

First, we have the woodpecker. The woodpecker
has an extremely sharp bill that is ideal for drilling
holes through the bark, enabling them to extract
juicy bugs from the tree. There are people in our
life who are just the same. They pick and pick and
pick away at the strength of our tree. They leave little
holes all over our spirit as they do their damage and

take from us what they need. Woodpeckers can be some of our most annoying influences. They can literally whittle us away with negativity.

Fungus and Disease

Oak trees can also be killed by fungus and disease. These spread from one tree to another, slowly creeping all over the tree until it can't breathe. Other pests feed off the fungus and eventually the great oak dies. People can do the same thing to us. They slowly spread their negative ideas into our minds and before we know it, they've infected us and other people around us. The negativity we feel from them feeds our anxiety, making it harder and harder to breathe. Eventually that fungus, that infection, kills our spirit. Many of us have had relationships or jobs like this. Some of us are still getting suffocated.

Insects

Oak trees can be killed by termites and other wood-eating insects. These insects are hidden and covert. Their damage may go unnoticed for some time and be quite extensive. Early detection and timely treatment are key in limiting damage. People and things in our lives can be just the same; eating away at our oak tree unbeknownst to us. This is often where things come into play, even more than people. We constantly surround ourselves with negative influences that subtly bring us down. Over time, they can do a lot of damage.

Storms

Oak trees can be lifted right out of the ground if the elements of a storm are just right. Mighty winds and natural disasters can easily uproot entire forests of strong and mighty oak trees. That's true for us in our lives. Death, loss, pain, financial failure, sickness, failed relationships—all these things are storms in our lives that can uproot our trees. In the blink of an eye, our trees can just disappear and we are left with a gaping, empty hole.

Fire

Fire also kills oak trees, reducing them to ashes. I have experienced many fires in my life. I have allowed others to affect my thinking and burn up my tree. What makes this the most painful is that you suffer the pain as the tree is burning. You are truly burning alive. You are left with nothing. You choose numbness and mundanely go back to what you call "life," forgetting you ever had a great oak tree and caring even less.

Every influence that has touched our lives has whittled away at our trees. Who and what is around us affect what we think, feel and do. It can impact what we eat, how we dress, what jobs we have, how we raise our kids, what we think of ourselves and our abilities, you name it. Some of us have had so many negative influences for so long that our trees have been whittled down to chopsticks. I know because I've been there several times in my life. I've been the chopstick, the toothpick, burned to ashes.

Change your influences and enhance your ability to focus on your own thoughts and feelings. Change your influences and speed your ability to maintain a positive attitude and spirit of thankfulness, thus changing your actions and getting closer to your goals. Break down those influences so you may give further thought to how these areas of your life are influencing you. Pay attention to who and what in your life are the termites, the fungus, the woodpeckers, the storms, and the fire.

Who is Influencing You?

Our parents or the people who raised us have helped shape who we are. For many of us, they continue to influence our thoughts about ourselves. Information from our parents has been feeding our hamster wheels for so long. Principles we learn from our primary caregivers have become facts in our minds. That doesn't make any of them true. It only makes them true to us. Whoever raised us imprinted us with ideas about ourselves that we may still believe.

When we attempt to forget the definitions of who we are that our parents have given us, a reminder from them will make us cringe with inadequacy. As I've said, I hold my mother's opinion in the highest regard. I'd listen to her advice second only to God's. My mom believes that a person should attend every family function. Family is important and sometimes we should attend events or do things for family members that require extra effort on our part. There are also moments when it is okay to say "no" to family so we can focus on ourselves.

On most occasions, I knew Mom was right. But as I grew older, I realized that given the size of my family and the distance between us, receiving an invitation didn't always mean I could go. Sometimes what was important to me and my wellness outweighed the need of the other person and I started saying "no." I didn't always find the same things as fun or as rewarding as my mom did. Our value systems for what made us feel good were different and that was okay. That didn't change how hard it is to say "no" or lessen the power of her influence.

If my mom suggests I attend one of these events that I don't want to go to but I know she wants me to, thoughts start running through my head. I attach to them feelings of guilt and behave in the negative. The process looks like this:

Mom says, "Are you going to the family reunion in August?"

I say, "Probably not."

She says, "You're not gonna go?"

Her response meant nothing; she was just asking a question that comes most naturally. In reality, she doesn't care if I do or if I don't go, but what I think and feel inside doesn't match that reality. As soon as she'd say it, I'd want to scream out, "No, I'm not going. You're the one who believes it's so important to be there. You go! I have no desire to go, there is no reason to go and I get no pleasure from going. I am not like you. I don't feel bad for not going.

Wait. Is there something wrong with me? She's probably right. Maybe I will feel bad if I don't go. It shouldn't be all about me. I should do this for her. If is it's important to her, I can just suck it up and get through it."

All these thoughts would spiral through my mind. Feelings of guilt and shame would flood over me and I'd do whatever was requested of me instead of what I wanted. Even when there wasn't pressure, I could find ways to apply it to myself in my mind. This would lead me to make the wrong decision about going and in many cases; I felt uncomfortable and did not have a good experience. I was allowing all my thoughts and emotions to mess up my ability to create a positive action. In time and with great practice, my mom and I have changed these thoughts, feelings and actions. I have learned that everything that comes from my Momma is from love. It is I who change the thoughts in my mind and add feelings to match. It's great to be giving and generous to others, but it's okay to give to ourselves, too.

This is just one example of how influences from others, such as our parents, play a huge role in who we are and how we behave. Parents influence us in a manner similar to how they were influenced by their parents. It's what they know, their level of awareness. How we are raised and how we are treated shapes how we influence others. We only pass on what we know. Every time my daughter says, "MOM!?!?" I wonder what her perception is of me and what I am passing on.

I can think of many things my parents say that make my mind go crazy. Has your parent ever made a comment to you that spiraled your thoughts and feelings into negative actions? Here are a few examples of harmless phrases that can produce quite a reaction... "You're gonna do that?" "You didn't do that?" "You should just think about this." "You know I'm only trying to help."

Some of us are so influenced by what our parents say that we follow every word. Others hide things from our parents and don't allow them to see the real us because we fear they won't fully accept it. We want them to maintain a certain image of us in their minds. We don't want to hear their criticism, because oftentimes, they are right. The feedback they give will only reinforce the many negative thoughts and feelings we already have.

Many of us have experienced seasons of financial hardship. When we are going through these tough times, some of us still spend money on things we shouldn't. And then the evidence of our spending comes to light. It only takes one comment like, "Oh Jim, with all the things you have on your plate and you guys got a new car? Are you sure that was best?" You were already wondering how you were going to afford the payments. You already have a lot of negative thoughts and feelings. That type of feedback from the people we love most can accelerate those negative emotions.

We all react to our parent's reactions. Your parents have and will continue to play a big part in feeding that oak tree and hamster wheel. Their impact is with us every day, even if they have moved on in spirit. The information in the hamster wheel does not stop until we stop it. If a parent told us we were fat, unworthy or ugly and they have since passed, there are plenty of reminders all around us that carry on their legacy of negativity. Only we can change the wheel.

A spouse or partner can be a huge influence in our circles, too. How we think, feel and act can be directly associated with our partners. Perhaps they are loving, supporting and always expressing love and adoration. Maybe they are absent, tired, overworked and neglectful. Whichever the case, your partner is directly influencing you right now. The type of relationship you have will depend on just how much of an influence your spouse or partner is.

From a young age growing up I had to wear glasses which had a huge impact on my self-esteem. The following story shares how these thoughts and feelings showed up in my relationship with my daughter's father. He was one of two great loves in my life so far and yet, his influence added to my negative thoughts and feelings, accelerating my negative actions.

When I was in 4th grade and about 9 years old, I got glasses for the first time. This was in the 1980s, which I'm sure was the ugliest decade we ever lived through in this country. And my glasses were just that — ugly. Two huge circles took up a good half of my face and my lenses were as thick as they were ugly. To top it off, the frames were light purple. Back then you could get the lenses tinted too and they were purple as well. I looked like I was wearing some type of fairy goggles. It was a disaster. I hated them when I put them on. And the first time I heard, "Four-eyes" or "You were prettier without glasses," it about broke me. Both are phrases that still send shivers down my spine.

A friend of mine at the time, Sharon, also wore glasses, a similar pair in blue. Three of us had to stay after school one day for an activity, Sharon, a boy from our class named Ryan, and me. We were hanging out in the room and Ryan started calling Sharon really ugly names, making fun of her and her glasses. Sharon got really scared and started to back away from Ryan. He backed her into the chalkboard, told her she was ugly and punched her square in the nose. I remember Sharon's face and the fear I felt watching it all take place. I remember the shock, Sharon screaming and Ryan laughing. I learned right there in that moment that not only were glasses ugly, they were dangerous.

I had contacts by the age of 14 and enjoyed the mild self-esteem boost they provided. I was so much more confident about how others saw me without glasses that I rarely wore them. They just made me feel ugly and undesirable. It wasn't long until I was abusing the privilege of contacts by not taking them out at night. I wore them much longer than I should have. I did not take care of my eyes at all through high school. In college, I fell in love with the man who would become the father of my daughter. One night while getting ready to go out to eat and watch a football game, I brushed mascara across my contact. No matter what I tried, I couldn't get the lens clean enough to wear without pain. I finally gave in since we were only going to watch a football game. It was just us on a Thursday night so I came out dressed and ready to go, wearing my glasses. When my sweetie turned around he said, "Aww, babe, you're gonna wear your glasses?" I remember the horrible feeling that came over me. Just like Ryan had punched Sharon in the face, my sweetie had just punched me. My entire countenance changed as I began to feel insecure about everything from my glasses to my outfit to my body size to my hair. I walked back into the bathroom and again tried to force the contact in my eye. Since I could not get it to stay in my eye comfortably, I took it out and only wore the left eye. I could barely see the entire night and ended up with a terrible headache.

The next day I went to the eye doctor and ordered a new pair of lenses. One week later, after only seeing from half my eyes I put in the new 6-week disposable pair. At the end of those 6 weeks, I could not afford another pair. The lack of self-esteem and the message spinning in my hamster wheel that glasses made me ugly was so strong that I wore the expired lenses for a full year. I never took them out, even to be cleaned. Nearing the end of that year, I awoke one morning to eyes that didn't want to open. Stumbling to the mirror, I got them open just wide enough to see redness. I knew I was in bad shape. I wasn't even sure how to get the lenses out. I had broken my glasses many months ago anyway so I decided to go to the eye doctor immediately. To no surprise I had done considerable damage to my eyes. My treatment plan included wearing glasses for a full year to heal all the damage I had done.

Thoughts lead to feelings; feelings lead to actions. All those thoughts still run in my hamster wheel. Even now I have issues and have to talk myself out of them. I had to learn that glasses did not define me or my beauty or desirability. They just helped me see. I had to change my thoughts to achieve happiness while wearing them. My sweetie didn't know the influence that one sentence had on me. The sweetie in your life now has no idea how they are influencing you.

If you have children you are also being influenced by them. Having a child that tells you they love you all day long, wants nothing but your love and is in perfect health, is a wonderful influence. But having the opposite as a parent can greatly affect your thoughts and attitudes. Your children are influencing you in some way.

We also have friends, sisters, brothers and many other people in our lives that have direct influences on our strengths and our weaknesses. Friends can encourage us to do things that aren't always what's best. Many of us try to better ourselves through diet and exercise. Knowing this, our friends are the first ones to invite us to the all-you-can-eat buffet, followed by ice cream and a movie marathon on the couch. Sometimes our friends, knowing we want to cut down on drinking, will invite us to a bar. They say, "Just have one and you'll be fine." Friends should love us for who we are and for all we want to be. Friends should always want better for us and support us when we're trying to obtain it. I hope each of us has friends like that.

It is crucial that we surround ourselves with people who are eager to lift us up and support any successes we achieve. Often our friends and closest family members are the first to knock us down when we express a new thought or idea. Fear usually drives the forces behind others when they reject our changes or our attempts to try something new. Fear is a very powerful force in the realm of emotions. That's a point that's been driven home for many of us over time and it shows up in many areas of our lives. These close influences affect your great oak tree and many of them are whittling away at you.

Besides our close family and friends, we have intricate bonds with other people in our social network. Some of us work for 8 hours a day in an office with the same people, day in and day out. Some of those environments are toxic to the spirit. They foster negative thoughts and feelings. It is easy to get caught up in the negative energy and be a negative Nellie yourself. New jobs can be very much like fungus or termites. It starts small, unseen, and before you know it, negativity is all over you and within you. I've seen many great people lose their positive spirit and steady oak tree to jobs that slowly take them over — myself included.

Some of the worst fungus and termites there are come from our worldly influences. The radio, television, Internet and all media offer you a constant stream of what's wrong in the world, and yet we tune in every morning for our daily update on how terrible the world is. It's a steady dose of death, hate, corruption and disease. We turn to shows that are filled with sex, violence and gut-wrenching drama. We flock to reality TV, feeling good as we watch others suffer or make fools of themselves. The more of these influences we expose ourselves to, the more those tree killers bury in your hamster wheel and kill your positive oak.

The Bible has a lot of great passages on this topic. Here are two:

> *Do not be misled: Bad company corrupts good character.*
> — *1 Corinthians 15:33 (NIV)*

> *Can a man walk on hot coals without his feet being scorched?*
> — *Proverbs 6:27 (NIV)*

What is around us affects us. What we have to do is learn to be our best selves. That means we have to put aside our influences, tune out the negative opinions around us and stop allowing ourselves to be poisoned by the world.

Who Are You Influencing?

My aunt, who is a preacher in my hometown, said something very powerful in her sermon recently. She said, "I myself don't know a prostitute, someone who openly denounces God. I've never met a murderer. I've probably met drug addicts and didn't know it, but in our area I've never been exposed to others who really need that love and God's light. If I did, I would show them, and that should make you all even more compelled to get out to all those in your community with much less problems and show them love. We must act on our love, for we all share in the same suffering. It all boils down to one thing: loneliness. We are all so truly lonely, especially those who don't know the constant company and love of our God."

Her words hit home with me so hard because I do know those people. I began to reflect on my journey in life so far and I realized that all along my path, God put countless suffering people there for me to love. Since I was a child, He had placed one person after another in line to challenge me and my ability to see them as diamonds in the rough. This calling and natural tendency of mine was quite difficult. It's not easy to love other people from the inside out when the world says you shouldn't love them. It's difficult to show forgiveness, kindness and compassion when others don't have the same capacity to see things as you do. It takes time to build up the courage to love them anyway and let what others say go in one ear and out the other. It took a long time for me to really step into that light. For the longest time, I thought something was wrong with me. I questioned my sanity at some points in my life as God allowed me to love people whom others would see as unlovable. I made many mistakes along the way. I ran from that calling on many occasions. To this day, I still think about those lessons and diligently try to grow from them.

When I was a child, I tried really hard to be nice to everyone. My heart would completely break when I saw another child being hurt or spoken harshly to. I was very emotional and felt compelled from within to reach out to those who were shunned or less popular. They seemed to matter to me. I have memories of these feelings as far back as kindergarten. There were a couple of students in particular in elementary school that I would even come home and tell my mom about. I badly wanted to help them feel better about who they were and do what I could to make them more accepted among our peers. This feeling continued inside me well into my high school years.

I had a dear friend in high school that I'll call John. He was not a popular kid; in fact he was what they'd call in my town a troublemaker. By middle school he was labeled a bad kid by the staff and the students. He got into fights all the time, didn't score well academically, wore the same clothes sometimes for days in a row and was generally feared and disliked. He had few friends, most of whom were family, and spent more time in suspension than in school. He may have even been expelled in high school.

From the moment I first remember meeting John, there was something about him I just adored. I had a genuine desire to get to know who he truly was. I couldn't believe that someone so angry and mean could shine such an amazing smile, joy beaming, eyes sparkling and not have something good inside. We dated for a short time, but soon realized we would make great friends instead. We didn't even kiss. We just spent a lot of time getting to know each other.

I learned that he had experienced a very rough life. His family was poor and a firm hand was used to raise him. He had taken many beatings for his behavior and had learned a life of fighting, struggle, pain and turmoil. The more I got to know him, the more I truly loved the little boy inside him who was yearning to be loved. I understood the anger that had been building in his life since he was young. His oak tree had been ripped from the ground numerous times. I saw that his anger, torment and rage was all just a mask to hide his pain, loneliness and fear. John was just a broken soul yearning for someone to love him.

I did my best through high school to honor our friendship and always stand up for him. It was hard to be his defender when everyone around me only saw the boy on the outside. I experienced my own pain as I struggled with my own sense of value. Being friends and defending someone like him often left me struggling for my value as others judged me and categorized my worth. After high school I made a poor choice and didn't answer the higher purpose I was being called to. It was a powerful lesson for me.

I had moved back home to Virginia to help my brother with his last semester of high school. I quickly reunited with an old friend of mine I had spent a lot of time with in high school, whose name was George. We had a lot in common and always made each other laugh. We had never been involved romantically; we were just really good friends. We'd even talk about who we were dating or interested in.

We began hanging out almost every night, including some weekends. I liked to go dancing at the Ramada Inn. It was the only thing to do in our small town if you were over 21. I had been there many times to dance and a lot of people I knew would be there, including John and sometimes George. I would spend the entire evening dancing to song after song. John was a great dancer and if he could stay out of trouble, not get drunk or kicked out, he would often spend the evening on the dance floor too. I even slow danced with him since I wasn't interested in any of the other guys. He was the only one that could keep a beat and keep his hands to himself. I always had fun when John was there.

George and I began to hang out more and more. One weekend, George suggested we go to the Ramada to dance, since I hadn't been there in a few weeks. I got ready and we headed out. When we got there I saw a lot of people I knew, including John. George also acknowledged John and gave me a look of disapproval. I felt very uncomfortable. George was one of my best friends. We spent so much time together and I cared about him very much. He was a good friend to me when others judged me and he always had my back. His disapproval was very hard on me and I struggled with what to do. I never ignored or was rude to John. I was always the one to dance with him and talk to him.

The feelings got worse and worse, so I had a few drinks and hit the dance floor. It wasn't long until John was dancing with me. As I let myself go and started having fun, I looked over and saw George just standing there looking at me funny. The longer I danced, the more disapproving George became. I didn't know how to react and within a few minutes, I sat down.

George was quickly by my side as if he was marking his territory. It didn't take him long to give his opinion on John and just what I looked like associating with him. He made me feel about two inches tall. I began to question how everyone in the room was looking at me and in that moment, it mattered to me. I could not answer the divine calling to stand up for John. I was too worried about my own value slipping.

George left me sitting alone to go talk to his friends. My mind continued to spiral in numerous directions. I felt so uncomfortable wondering what everyone was thinking and feeling. In high school, George and I were friends behind the scenes. No one really knew how much we talked or hung out. Now I was at the Ramada with George. People finally started looking at me a little different, judging me less. I didn't know what to do or think. The next song that played was a slow song. John came to my table to ask me to dance.

Like a coward, lost in fear and loneliness I said, "No, not this one." I had never said no to him before. Why would I? I had never let anyone stand in my way before and I had no reason to now, but something wouldn't let me say yes. He looked at me like

I was crazy and slowly stepped back, deeply hurt by my answer and my expression. I realized within seconds that George was now standing next to me exchanging negative looks with John. In the blink of an eye I had hurt three very important people — God, John, and myself. I knew right away it was wrong and hung my head in shame. I was overcome with regret and George and I left soon after.

I didn't go back to the Ramada Inn and I didn't continue spending much time with George. Instead, I focused on my work and planned my next move. John was often on my mind and shortly before I moved away, I ran into him in town. When he saw me coming, he looked at me differently. He looked at me like he looked at everyone else — guarded and angry. He was cold and distant and no longer saw me as a source for unconditional love. I did my best to explain how stupid I had been and apologized over and over. I knew he forgave me and that he believed my sincerity, but it couldn't repair the damage that had been done.

I have thought about John for years. I pondered where he was and what he was doing. Did he find happiness? I prayed for his success and that he would find all the things he dreamed, despite the hard life he had known. He crossed my mind often and I was thrilled in 2011 to see him on Facebook. I quickly friended him and we made small talk to catch up. We didn't stay in contact, but it was nice seeing his face every now and then. I watched him fall in and out of love. I saw him struggle with his feelings and the circumstances around him. I enjoyed seeing pictures of him and his kids and I believed that despite all his pain, he was ok. No matter how much time passed, I still thought about that night at the Ramada and had a deep feeling of sadness. For years I internally beat myself up over how I treated John that evening.

In the middle of May 2012, I got an overwhelming feeling to call him, to reach out and say how sorry I was again. I needed to make things right for myself as I could not believe the amount of shame I still carried after 14 years. I shared this desire with my friend Jen and then completely ignored the calling to reach out to John. I was so busy and focused on what mattered around me that I didn't listen to what mattered within me.

One month later on June 9, 2012 I was devastated to find out that John committed suicide.

I was upset for days. I wished so badly I had listened to my internal messenger and reached out and said something, even just hello. You don't get another chance to say tomorrow what you should have said today. John left this world in pain, suffering inside, abandoned and alone. I started thinking about other people in my life who were like John. There were so many. My boyfriend at the time was an intense version of John. I had been with him for 8 years on and off. Not only was he a man I loved very much, he was also a man who had given me endless knowledge on how truly miserable people think, feel and act. When my sweetie would enter fits of rage that would leave most people on the phone with 911, I knew exactly what to do. Over time, I learned so much that I was easily able to manage his anger and rage and operate at a level that allowed my sweetie to exit the negative feelings and resume normal thinking, feelings and behaviors. Most of the time, this rage is just fear and pain all mixing together in a violent storm. The emotions that have been pushed down over time come flooding to the surface and it is very much like an explosion. This can be seen in people at all sorts of levels.

About 2 weeks after John killed himself, I started to think about another lost soul I spent time with in high school. Billy was a boy I dated for a while that I was quite caught up with. People judged how he dressed, his friends and the music he listened to; no one could understand why I would like such a guy. I, however, was completely lost in him. We would lie in his room for hours and talk. He was so beautiful to me. Listening to him talk was like listening to his soul sing. He was a dreamer. Like John, he had lived a rough life and was always in trouble.

I got a great urge to reach out to him, but had no clue how to find him. I mentioned this to my friend Jen as well. John's death had made me curious to see where this other friend was. Had he battled his way through the darkness to happiness? Like John, he had little support or encouragement.

I could not find him anywhere and gave up my search. On July 9, 2012, exactly 30 days after John's suicide, Billy, requested to friend me on Facebook. I was completely in awe and looked at the dates over again and again. I didn't have to go looking for Billy. He found me.

Within moments of his request, we emailed back and forth. He was not well. He gave me no details, just that his heart had been completely broken and the fault was in his own bad choices. He said he was trying so hard to be a better person, but he wasn't perfect and messed up sometimes. I told him I had been thinking of him and that I always thought he had a beautiful soul. I assured him everything would be okay.

He wanted to attend my motivational seminar that weekend in his hometown, but didn't have a ride. I thought about picking him up, but had no idea how to work it out and didn't even offer. I said a few more encouraging words and left it alone. I didn't know how involved to get. I didn't want to upset a girlfriend or wife. Even though I meant no harm and had my own life and sweetie, reaching out and offering my friendship could be misinterpreted. I would never want more trouble or pain for anyone involved in anything. I've had enough of my own.

I got on his Facebook page and started to look around. Judging by all his posts and pictures, it was obvious this was a man that was hurting. It was clear that he was going through several battles in his life and that he carried terrible shame and guilt. It was clear he was lonely and broken, consumed in negative thoughts and feelings. It was also clear his actions had continued to back it all up. He posted on my page for the next few days, shared my event pages, and liked all my posts. I never got to back to Billy, though I thought about him almost every day. I was so busy and focused on what mattered around me that I didn't listen to what mattered within me.

On July 20, 2012, he was shot and killed by police in a domestic incident in our hometown. The last words Billy said to me were, "Your friend always…" Those words kept my head spinning over the next few days. My thoughts were not just about Billy, not just about John, but all the lost and hurting souls. I've been through so much pain in the last few years that I'm one of them too. We're all out here hurting, but we take that pain and hurt each other.

John and Billy had extreme amounts of negative thoughts and feelings. In fact, they were on overload with those intense thoughts and feelings all the time. From the time they were young, their hamster wheels were fed negative, limiting, inaccurate information. They learned their identities and values from who and what surrounded them. The ways others treated them continued to foster more negative thoughts and feelings, further establishing their identities. Their thought highways had dozens of lanes, all consumed by chaos, accidents and long rest stops. Their oak trees had been uprooted, burnt down, eaten up and suffocated so many times they didn't believe their trees existed any more. They couldn't trust in anything or anyone.

All along this process, their negative actions and behaviors also became stronger and stronger. They made bad choices and negative decisions; they struggled with a lot of things many of us find easy. But it's not all their fault. I hold us all responsible. Each and every one of us has a responsibility to love and reach out to the Johns and the Billys of this world. These are the people who need our generosity and love. These are the people whose spirits are broken and so richly deserve our support and understanding. I've often said that what you judge and don't understand will only show up in your life to teach you the lessons you couldn't see without the experience.

Bringing Sunshine To The Forest

Let me tell you why you are here. You're here to be salt-seasoning that brings out the God flavors of this earth. If you lose your saltiness, how will people taste godliness? You've lost your usefulness and will end up in the garbage. Here's another way to put it: You're here to be light, bringing out the God colors in the world. God is not a secret to be kept. We're going public with this, as public as a city on a hill. If I make you light-bearers, you don't think I'm going to hide you under a bucket, do you? I'm putting you on a light stand. Now that I've put you there on a hilltop, on a light stand — SHINE!! Keep open house; be generous with your lives. By opening up to others, you'll prompt people to open up with God, this generous father in heaven.

— *Matthew 5:13-15* (MSG)

Do you get the power in those verses? I get chills as I write this for you. We have a direct assignment all of us.

> *And he said to him, "You shall love the*
> *Lord your God with all your heart and with all*
> *your soul and with all your mind. This is the*
> *great and first commandment. And a second is*
> *like it: You shall love your neighbor as yourself."*
> *—Matthew 22:37-39 (ESV)*

We are supposed to love God with all our hearts first. That's our number one assignment. We know that means loving ourselves, too. We are of God. We are His divine creation. His blood is flowing through us. We are His children. He is asking us to love ourselves too, first. Through that love, that positive outlook and attitude, that thankfulness, we are whole. We are complete. Then and only then can we reach our second assignment and love others with the unconditional love they so richly yearn for and deserve.

God knows that our ability to complete those two assignments can be affected by who and what are around us. I love this passage too:

> *How well God must like you; you don't*
> *hang out at Sin Saloon, you don't slink along*
> *Dead End Road, you don't go to Smart-Mouth*

> *College. Instead you thrill to God's word; you*
> *chew on Scripture day and night. You're a tree*
> *replanted in Eden, bearing fresh fruit every*
> *month. Never dropping a leaf, always in bloom.*
> — *Psalms 1:1-3*(MSG)

That's two amazing promises he's made to us in those two Scripture passages. This divine way of living, expecting miracles where tragedy falls, seeing the beauty in ourselves and others, giving glory and thanks for all we have, gets us a replanted tree. A new one. A fresh oak to work with. Our God is a generous God and following His assignments will lead us to great evidence of this generosity.

> *But blessed is the man who trusts me, God,*
> *the woman who sticks with God. They're like*
> *trees replanted in Eden, putting down roots near*
> *the rivers- Never a worry through the hottest of*
> *summers, never dropping a leaf, serene and calm*
> *through droughts, bearing fresh fruit every season.*
> — *Jeremiah 17: 7-8* (MSG)

I want that for everyone reading this book. Taking action to change how things influence us is a major step in our shared journey. Don't worry about what others have to say. They'll want to be a part of the magic. Or, our circles of influence will change to match the circles we should have.

It's important to me that I be clear here. Every story or example is not to place blame, pain or responsibility for who we are. We each do what we can with what we know. Awareness is something all of us need more of. Our parents did what they were taught to do to the best of their ability and we do the same. In so many cases, people just don't know any other way. There is no blame to be placed on changes that need to be made. Things we learn about ourselves through others is what it is. Each of us are held responsible for ourselves. We allow information to influence our imagination. We use information to influence others' imaginations. Change is ours alone; blame goes nowhere. Nothing gives us an excuse to project negative energy onto others.

The Oak Tree Protection Program

To Throw the Stone

Jesus went across to Mount Olives, but he was soon back in the Temple again. Swarms of people came to him. He sat down and taught them.

The religious scholars and Pharisees led in a woman who had been caught in an act of adultery. They stood her in plain sight of everyone and said, "Teacher, this woman was caught red-handed in the act of adultery. Moses, in the Law, gives orders to stone such persons. What do you say?" They were trying to trap him into saying something incriminating so they could bring charges against him.

Jesus bent down and wrote with his finger in the dirt. They kept at him, badgering him.

He straightened up and said, "The sinless one among you, go first: Throw the stone." Bending down again, he wrote some more in the dirt. Hearing that, they walked away, one after another, beginning with the oldest. The woman was left alone. Jesus stood up and spoke to her. "Woman, where are they? Does no one condemn you?"

"No one, Master."

"Neither do I," said Jesus. "Go on your way. Behave better."

—*John 8:1-11 (MSG)*

What a powerful lesson we learn in this story from the Bible. Everyone struggles. Everyone faces challenges and battles. Everyone makes mistakes. Each of us has a list of bad choices and dumb decisions we have made along our journeys. We are all equal, regardless of the level of these negative choices. One cannot say they have suffered more than another. All pain is pain and it hurts for everyone. You can not measure to what degree each person experiences it.

Yet in the world we live in, so many people are anxious to get out the rock launchers. We don't just throw stones in this generation. We have built giant machines that hoist enormous boulders into the air to crush our opponents. We cause pain and suffering for fun. We gossip, make assumptions and judge people all the time. People judge one another on dozens of levels; how much they have, how they live, their choices, behaviors and past. The movies you've created in your hamster wheel about others play over and over in our imaginations and foster more negative judgment.

The judgment process usually begins with physical appearance. We make assumptions about others based on their clothes, hair color and body shape. Think about the popular phrase: "Dress for Success." The world says you need to look good and well put together to be smart, talented and successful. This is far from true. We can be successful naked, wearing only a pair of fancy flip-flops, with the right thinking. The opposite is only true because society has set such a standard. We feel a drop in our value when we don't measure up to it.

Youth who don't have the latest styles from the coolest stores struggle to fit in with the kids who do. Those who do are considered more popular, desirable people. This limited thinking carries over into our adulthood and is all around us. Worldly influences set up a value system for us based on what we look like and we enforce it. So many struggle to keep up, buy the next thing, wear the best clothes in the hope of making ourselves feel more of value in the world. We are already more valuable to the world. without the appearance and those things. I love this quote:

If most of us are ashamed of shabby clothes
and shoddy furniture let us be more ashamed
of shabby ideas and shoddy philosophies.... It
would be a sad situation if the wrapper were
better than the meat wrapped inside it.
— *Albert Einstein*

We have to look at the meat that's wrapped inside. That's a powerful quote. Collecting material objects is where we begin collecting our stones, piling them up against others. We judge people on appearance and material possessions long before we express an interest in getting to know the person within. This goes both ways, since there is a good chance that someone is also judging us. Thoughts about someone's appearance leads to assumptions about their character and life. For example, many people I know judge others who have tattoos. They automatically categorize people with tattoos and label them with certain assumptions. We establish an outline of a person before we ever get to know them. Often this outline in our imagination is enough to prevent us from getting to know them at all. We don't even give them a chance. This process we've created in disabling our ability to really "see" each other has also broken down our ability to really love each other. We instead create more warfare and turmoil in our thinking, feelings and actions.

Often when broken people are suffering, the people closest to them inflict even more damage. They break us down at warp speed and sometimes don't even realize it. I've done it myself. I had a boyfriend cheat on me. I chose to forgive him and move on. I knew he beat himself up about it every time he looked at me. I watched him cringe with guilt and shame when the subject would come up, yet I reminded him of it and beat him up with it every chance I could. I was like an axe chopping away at him, making him feel the pain. And why? Did this make me feel better about myself? No.

A broken person feels even worse about themselves when the people they love tear them down. For me, at the time I focused only on the cheating, which led to intense feelings and crippling actions. To change the results, I should have focused on a healthy relationship and the good feeling generated by that thought. I may still have had ill feelings toward the cheating, but would have been working to get past it by changing the only thing I could — myself. Only we can control how we think, feel and act. I didn't use what I knew to make it better. I should have just walked away because those thoughts and feelings I couldn't control led to actions that just caused further damage to us both.

In another sermon I heard my Aunt Diane preach, she said that we have to do more than offer prayer. That's generally the extent of what we do.

We offer prayer for one another. Please don't get me wrong: There is tremendous power in prayer, but that is just the beginning of what we can do for one another. Prayer is just one powerful source of healing and restoration. Reaching out to one another, stepping past all the judgments and into the light of compassion and service is not a choice many of us make. We follow the crowd. We feel bad or sorry for that person, but it is rare that we put ourselves out there and get our hands dirty.

Our society breaks us down, so we need to offer more than our prayers to those in need. The broken need others to reach out and make them feel needed, wanted and alive. They need to believe people can see the diamond within them, not just their past or current situation and rough exterior. They need unconditional love, not to be thrown under the bus. For many years, my mother questioned my judgment on who I spent time with and felt sincere feelings for. Many of the people I shared myself with had a terrible image on the outside and had been through serious circumstances. But the light I could see within them was strong and very real. I never saw their situations, their past or their material worth. I never assumed their outside demeanor was a complete reflection of who they were. I was always capable of seeing the light beyond it and finding the source of pain that caused the negative thinking and behavior. It is a gift I have only recently learned to understand and embrace. I feel like the luckiest person in the world to have it.

If all of us reached out and showed a little kindness to the next person, the world would change as rapidly as our own lives. If all of us reached out a hand a little farther to the suffering people around us, we would give and receive great healing. If all of us worked together to love, to support and lift up the Johns and Billys of the world, we may not save them all, but I'm sure we'd make a pretty good dent in the mountain of pain and misery. As our light shines from within onto another, we are then blessed with that light in return. None of us can cast the first stone, so put the rocks down and learn how to really love one another.

> *"To you who are ready for the truth, I say this: Love your enemies. Let them bring out the best in you, not the worst. When someone gives you a hard time, respond with the energies of prayer for that person. If someone slaps you in the face, stand there and take it. If someone grabs your shirt, giftwrap your best coat and make a present of it. If someone takes unfair advantage of you, use the occasion to practice the servant life. No more tit-for-tat stuff. Live generously.*
>
> *"Here is a simple rule of thumb for behavior: Ask yourself what you want people to do for you; then grab the initiative and do*

it for them! If you only love the lovable, do you expect a pat on the back? Run-of-the-mill sinners do that. If you only help those who help you, do you expect a medal? Garden-variety sinners do that. If you only give for what you hope to get out of it, do you think that's charity? The stingiest of pawnbrokers does that.

"I tell you, love your enemies. Help and give without expecting a return. You'll never — I promise — regret it. Live out this God-created identity the way our Father lives toward us, generously and graciously, even when we're at our worst. Our Father is kind; you be kind.

"Don't pick on people, jump on their failures, criticize their faults — unless, of course, you want the same treatment. Don't condemn those who are down; that hardness can boomerang. Be easy on people; you'll find life a lot easier. Give away your life; you'll find life given back, but not merely given back — given back with bonus and blessing. Giving, not getting is the way. Generosity begets generosity."

He quoted a proverb: "'Can a blind man guide a blind man?' Wouldn't they both end up in the ditch? An apprentice doesn't lecture the master. The point is to be careful who you follow as your teacher.

"It's easy to see a smudge on your neighbor's face and be oblivious to the ugly sneer

on your own. Do you have the nerve to say,
'Let me wash your face for you,' when your own
face is distorted by contempt? It's this I-know-
better-than-you mentality again, playing a
holier-than-thou part instead of just living your
own part. Wipe that ugly sneer off your own
face and you might be fit to offer a washcloth to
your neighbor."

— *Luke 6:27-42* (MSG)

The thoughts we have churning in our hamster wheels combined with our influences dramatically impact our lives. Thoughts lead to feelings. Feelings lead to actions. Actions lead back to thoughts and the cycle can be maddening.

Have you ever had a really bad day? I have days when I wear something out of the house I think looks better than it really does. Its not until 5:00 p.m. and I'm leaving work that I catch my reflection in my car. Suddenly I realized there's an embarrassing tear in my pants right on my behind. I thought the pants were too tight, but made it through the day thinking I had no problem. And of course, everyone saw that tear in my pants and no one had said a word all day. I taught several classes and had seen nearly 100 different people that day. The embarrassment of this situation would have me spiraling at the end of the day. Reviewing facts and times through the day reaffirmed my embarrassment and shame. By the time I arrive home, I am a mess, totally embarrassed, fuming that no one said anything, mortified inside. Have you ever had one of those days?

Those thoughts and feelings mix together to create havoc within the body. That havoc or stress needs to be managed. Our bodies want us to feel good. They have internal chemistry supporting them. Since that's the case, on a day like this, our bodies will encourage us to do something that makes us feel good. They will call out for one of our favorite negative behaviors. Until we teach the hamster wheel to control our negative thoughts and emotions, we will likely respond with a negative behavior.

I know a lot of people who after a day like this would reach for a sugary treat, a cookie or piece of cake, some kind of snack to temporarily relieve the negative feeling. Eating that snack would cause more thought. How can you split your pants and then eat cookies? That thought would spiral into a matching negative feeling of shame and guilt and chances are we would eat more cookies. Change the cookie to any addiction. When we have unhealthy thoughts and feelings, unhealthy behaviors follow, leading only to a repeat of this cycle.

Actions

What we think and how we feel ends up in our actions. What we do every day with all we're thinking and feeling is a great stress on our bodies, which have all the tools necessary to help us reduce stress. When it comes to our physical actions and our behaviors, our brains and natural instincts want us to be happy. Our brains are set up with functions that encourage happiness. Happiness directly affects our brains' ability to manage hunger, our feelings of satisfaction, or cravings for things both good and bad. Happiness naturally affects our addictions with food, sex, smoking, gambling, shopping and alcohol, to name a few. Happiness and joy sit at the top of the ladder of success.

The brain has an entire structure devoted to our emotions, called the limbic system or emotional brain. This structure works with our digestive system in managing our needs for food. It also manages our reward systems, regulates consciousness and does many other amazing things. It's an area of the body we all should learn more about.

When it comes to being happy, there are 2 important neurotransmitters in the brain that I want to teach you about. A neurotransmitter is a very general term for any chemical signal that the brain sends. The first is serotonin. I call it "happy juice" because it's so exciting and we all have it. And what makes it even more exciting? It's free! How would you like an unlimited supply of happy juice? You'd love it. Many people spend lots of money on pre-scription medications, illegal substances, alcohol or gambling to imitate the effects of the happy juice. But they can access this for free.

Serotonin's job is to help regulate our mood and activate the parts of our brain that make us happy. We need good attitudes and thankful spirits in order to keep making a lot of it! We want it surging through our bodies, sending messages to our brains to release happiness. The more serotonin we produce, the more easily we ward off addictions. It's crucial to fuel and move our bodies to increase the production of sero-tonin. We'll talk more about that a little later.

Happy juice, or serotonin, is not the only good thing going for us in our brains. Dopamine is another neurotransmitter that works with the limbic system to manage our reward systems. Of all the things I learned about the brain in the past 12 years, dopamine is my personal favorite. It's like having a personal cheerleader living inside ourselves. This cheerleader encourages us to get the things that feel good to us, and then get more of them. Dopamine is a tool that few of us have learned to use correctly. It has been working since we were born to connect us with what feels good. It's made connections to food, alcohol, people and places. It's connected to everything we love.

Here's an example to explain the connection between dopamine and food addiction:

When you fell at Grandma's house as a child, you were conditioned to respond a certain way. Grandma would scoop you up and sit you on the counter. She'd have your wound clean and a Band-Aid on it within a few minutes. But the real healing and dopamine connection wasn't the Band-Aid. Grandma would sit you on a chair and give you a cookie and milk. She'd hug you and talk softly, easing your emotions. That is where dopamine got its cue. Dopamine found great pleasure in the cookie, the milk and your grandma. These things brought you comfort and made you feel good.

Because we are all adults now and don't have a kindly grandmother on hand when we are feeling low, we often turn to the cookie instead. The good feeling we got really came from Grandma, not the cookie, but dopamine saw the cookie as a reward, a pleasure. Dopamine believes cookies can cure our hurt feelings. We've been reinforcing that message to the hamster wheel for a long time.

So many Americans battle addictions. With some thought, we can trace back what has been fed to the hamster wheel and why we have many of those attachments. If we love a certain restaurant, there is an emotional reason besides the food. If we smoke, there is an emotional reason along with the nico-tine. If we have any addictions, there are emotional reasons attached to them and dopamine is what tells us it feels good and that we need to have more of it.

I have had many addictions myself. It took years to figure out my attachment to many of the foods in my life. One by one, memories came flooding back and I can now put a memory to almost every food I feel I cannot live without. Gibble's potato chips were a staple on my grocery list. There are dozens of better chips, but they taste the best to me because they have a connection to my own grandma. They make me feel good when I eat them. They soothe me and there are lots of others.

Because dopamine wants us to de-stress and feel rewarded, it will do anything, positive or negative, as long as it feels we are getting pleasure. Look at smoking. I smoked for 20 years. Besides my nicotine addiction, I had a neurotransmitter in my brain, reinforcing the belief that I needed those smokes. And one was never enough. Dopamine always pushed me to have more. Changing my thoughts and feelings, understanding my connection to the cigarettes, simply becoming *aware* changed everything. I realized that I was healthy and smoking didn't fit into a healthy lifestyle. I used those words every day, even when I was smoking. Over time, the smokes became less desirable to me. I realized that smoking was essentially like taking a break to breathe deeply and relax. I was just adding a cancer stick to the mix. I learned to change my thoughts and feelings, and then my actions changed too. I started taking "breathing breaks." In a few days I was past the nicotine addiction and sure enough, I don't smoke today. Do I still have to work to maintain this, yes. We are all human and it takes a lot of time and effort, but it can be done. When you fail, you get up and start again.

We could discuss a number of different addictions, but they all come down to this: Garbage in equals garbage out. Pretty simple stuff. As we learned earlier with influences, who and what is around us affects us. In the following section, let's look at how this works in several areas of our lives. Each section will show us how we can make small changes toward becoming healthier mental, emotional and physical beings.

Rise And Shine

The first few hours of the day are of the highest importance. They set the tone for the entire day and start the wheels of thought turning. What we think when we open our eyes is crucial to establishing a positive outlook. Most of us open our eyes right back to the worries we shut off the night before. Whatever was on our plates last night comes spiraling right back through our minds as we make a list of things we have to get done, problems that are bothering us, worries we cannot control. It used to be that by the time I got myself from the bed to the bathroom, I was already on mental overload. Waking up was something I just couldn't stand to do. I was grouchy and irritated. I didn't feel rested and surely never felt excited about the day ahead. Even things I truly looked forward to could be turned around by my negative thinking. My thoughts would be spiraling out of control before I ever left the house in the morning.

Not only would I open my eyes and return to negative thinking, I absorbed myself in it. After pouring my coffee, I would turn on the news. I would listen for at least 30 minutes about all the negative events taking place in my community, my country and the world. I watched stories of death and loss. I felt fear and anxiety as I listened to reports on government, crime and the economy. I felt tremendous sympathy for the victims of accidents, murders, natural disasters or kidnappings. I bathed my mind in negative thinking and spread that news and information to others at work. We would talk and discuss turmoil and loss. I couldn't get those graphic images out of my mind.

The day I stopped tuning in for my morning dose of pain, loss and destruction truly began to change my life–just that one little thing. Many said to me, "How can you not stay in tune with the world?" My answer to that is, "How can you?" Why would any of us want to fill our minds with this information? We all know it's going on; why tune in for a detailed recap? What good does it really serve us? Important information that we ought to know will easily reach us throughout our day.

We can offer prayer, support and love to all the individuals on the daily news without watching it and letting our minds absorb the images and hear the words. Sports, weather, and most community news can be found from other sources. We can select which stories to read and which stories to skip.

As if the news wasn't enough, I had plenty of other ways to begin my day on the wrong foot. I spent years dealing with betrayal after betrayal. I stayed in many negative relationships, trying to master the art of forgiveness, while forgetting the necessity of self-preservation. Fortitude, my friend Linda called it—the ability to maintain great strength while enduring great pain. Looking back, I see it as one of my greatest weaknesses.

A few years ago, there was no trust in my relationship. My mind was saturated with doubt and fear. From the moment I awoke, I wondered where he had been the night before, what I would find in his email, who would contact me that day, what could happen to leave me broken and empty again. The feeling of fear and madness would hit so fast that by the time I walked from the bed to the bathroom I was sick. Before I could sit down, I would have my phone open and begin searching through every avenue to catch him.

I would fill my mind with images and conversations that caused me great pain. I would search for him everywhere on the internet, analyze the profile of every friend he had on Facebook, and check Facebook accounts of everyone he had ever cheated on me with. I was nuts. That thought process followed me throughout my entire day—more thoughts leading to more feelings and more actions. I reached a point where I checked my phone and these sources dozens of times a day. I could not function without an update of each area I believed I could catch him through, searching for evidence to give me another chance to make a different choice. I lived this way for years, feeding my hamster wheel with betrayal and fear. It didn't serve me or my relationship well.

When we arise in the morning, it is one of the most important times in the day. Be sure to fill it with things that make you happy. Be sure to begin with a positive attitude and thankfulness.

The Road Trip

Ever notice that anyone going slower than you is an idiot, but anyone going faster is a maniac?

Two hundred twenty million of us are in our cars for an average of an hour and a half per day. That is a lot of time spent in the car. People behind the wheel of a car can become aggressive, angry and even hostile. Careless drivers cause accidents all the time. Most of us are guilty of speeding or not following a driving rule or two every now and then.

I have read that as many as one-third of us are considered aggressive drivers and some of us can even respond with road rage, which is described as violent anger caused by the stress and frustration involved in driving a motor vehicle. That says a lot for how driving affects all of us. Whether the person with road rage or the victim of it, a lot can be changed about how we think, feel and act behind the wheel.

I was that aggressive driver for many years. I would scream and yell and carry on. I would speed beyond the limit to abusive levels and blare my emotionally driven music. I would cuss, throw the middle finger, beep the horn and be hostile to anyone on the road not driving according to my standards. Nothing got under my skin worse than someone merging onto the highway at 45 mph. I would ride their bumper all the way down the ramp, ranting and raving the whole way. My mother would always tell me how scared she was to get on the highway because she knew that behind her there was someone like me, having a fit. And she was right. I was rude to other drivers. I was reckless and ungrateful for the incredible privilege driving really is.

I remember when my daughter began to mimic me from the back seat. She was very young when she made the greatest impression on me by acting just like me and flipping the middle finger. Within moments of her actions my awareness increased and I realized I needed to apply all I had learned about thinking and feeling to my behavior in the car. I quickly realized how my day could easily turn negative after a frustrating ride to work. It occurred to me that even the songs I tuned into were fueling my emotions. There were so many songs I could connect to my turmoil and they fueled my emotions even more, dumping thoughts and feelings into the hamster wheel.

After watching my daughter imitate my behavior in the car, I began to think about what I could change to make driving a more positive experience. After making small changes in my thoughts, I began to see a huge change in how I felt in the car. I've turned driving into another piece of life I can use to fuel my highest self.

When stepping into a vehicle, evaluate before you operate. I've gotten into my car so many times when I shouldn't have. I have been filled with rage before I ever turned the ignition key. I have been screaming with tears as I've sped away. I have driven with emotion and that is a huge mistake for both driver and passenger. Take time for a few deep breaths and some focus. Shake off whatever it is you're feeling before you ever begin. Always play a positive movie of your drive. Use your mind to see a journey filled with safety and positivity. Imagine that each car on the road with you is your neighbor. Leave enough time in your travels to show kindness to other drivers. They'll never see you coming! View the road blocks, traffic jams and cars that are moving slowly as angels that are there to further guide your journey. Find thankfulness in all that is happening around you, whether it presents itself as positive or not. The person who cut you off could be the person involved in the traffic accident at the very next light.

If you are in your car for more than a few minutes, be sure what you listen to positively fuels you.

If you hear a song that makes you feel anger, sadness, despair or loss, change the station. If the news comes on, change the station. Gravitate towards stations and CDs that lift you up, music that makes you feel good and calm. Try listening to books or inspirational materials on CD. Make your ride an uplifting time for your mind and offer yourself the opportunity to control your thoughts, feelings and actions.

Be sure your vehicle is an environment that makes you feel good. Having a dirty car with trash all over the floor, dust and dirt in the carpet and upholstery, will affect how you feel. Take some time each week to remove any trash and clutter from your vehicle. A clean space is good for the spirit. If you are in a hurry or late, the first thing you should do is slow down. Slowing down puts you in more control of your thoughts, feelings and actions.

Feed Your Spirit

Pray / Meditate

Prayer or meditation time will help feed the spirit. It is crucial to find time every day to just be quiet and receive. All too often, prayer time becomes a list of what's wrong and what we need. Make prayer time about thankfulness, about being quiet enough to hear God sharing with you, gently guiding you toward where He wants you to go. He knows everything you need, everything you want. Just come in the quiet, being there only to enjoy His presence. Great things will happen in this quiet time.

Praise / Worship

Find ample time each day to praise or worship. It's crucial to live from that divine place of happiness and appreciation, and praise or worship time is a great way to do that. It can lift you up out of your darkest moments. When the world is crashing

Actions

around you, when there is no doorway in sight to
walk through, throw your hands up and praise! Sing
a song you know. Yell out words of thankfulness.
Put on good music and dance. These times offer
great strength and joy within, despite the darkness
of our reality. Find time every day to praise.

You Are What You Eat

Most of my connections to food involve my grandparents. I lost my mother's mom on Christmas Eve in 1986, a void I have been filling ever since. My attachments and detachments to food began then. I suffered from anorexia for many years, reaching my lowest weight of 85 pounds over 10 years ago. I battled this disease for many years. When I learned I was pregnant, I became a compulsive eater overnight and gained 100 pounds with my pregnancy. The battle with my body continued for years after my pregnancy as I lost the weight and strove for perfection.

I've learned through many years of experience that for me, food was about feeling, not fueling. It's a major problem, just like any other addiction. It ranks up there with alcohol, smoking and drugs. Sugar is a drug and it controls many of us.

If we are what we eat, then we are a mess. It's projected that nearly 75% of the population in the United States will be overweight or obese by 2020. That statistic tells us that food addiction is a major consequence of negative thought. Look around. Negative thought is all around us and it's contagious like a disease. We have learned to use food to help make us "feel" better about our bad days, our bad relationships, our bad jobs, our bad lives. We have turned food and eating into a recreational sport. Eating is a hobby. We wake, we work, we eat and we sleep. Eating has its own distinguished place in our lives. Our passion for calories isn't the only problem; it's the lack of quality in those calories.

Fifteen million of us eat McDonald's every day. We consume 475 calories a day in *added* sugar, which equals 30 teaspoons or 30 packets of sugar. The average American consumes 180 pounds of sugar per year. Collectively, we drink 100 million gallons of cola per day.

Food, originally designed for survival and not just pleasure, has taken over the world. Our ancestors had as few as 12 items per week to choose from to eat. We have giant stores with a vast variety of food options. These great advances come at a cost, since many of those options are junk to our bodies. We are swimming in refined sugar and our diets are as poor as our thinking. Marketing companies have done their research and they know us intimately. They are masters at turning any item into a feel-good food. When's the last time a Betty

Crocker commercial didn't give you that warm and fuzzy feeling?

To be sure we gravitate to these feel–good items, stores put the healthiest items the furthest from our price range. You can feed a family a meal from a box with little to no nutritional value for under $7, but add up some fresh organic vegetables, an organic meat of choice with some brown rice and you're looking at spending no less than $15 to $20.

Going out to eat can be worse. Our portion sizes have increased as much as 75%. We are eating meals that are packed with as many as 4000 to 6000 calories. That's enough for 3 people for a day. Restaurants and fast food joints go the extra mile by advertising the concept that their food makes you feel something. They've turned food into an experience. Remember, we are designed to be fueled, not fed.

Not only do we have an obesity problem, we have a vast health problem. There is more at stake here than pant size and the effects on our self–image. The average American consumes:

- Half of the RDA of fiber
- Double the RDA of sodium
- Triple the RDA of trans fats

There are terrible consequences to this poor eating. We are being overtaken by diseases like cancer, diabetes and heart conditions. The list is outrageous. One condition leads to another condition, and so on and so on. So we treat these problems with pills, which cause side effects, which require yet more pills to treat. It's a vicious cycle and also impacts our thoughts. We are consumed by feelings of sickness and a lack of well-being. Disease can take over our minds and encourage more diseases.

It is time to stand up in this country and demand a change. How we fuel our bodies will greatly affect how we feel emotionally. What we eat affects our serotonin and dopamine levels, and we need them working for us, not against us.

You are what you eat. As you sit down to eat, change the way you think about food. Stop using it as an action to your thoughts and feelings. When you are eating, ask yourself a question. Is this business or pleasure? Food should be about business, fueling the body so that it may continue to thrive for you. You need to stick to lean meats and fish, fresh fruits and veggies, low-fat dairy choices, whole grains, and herbs and spices instead of salt.

There are many things we can do to fuel our bodies more efficiently. The best thing we can do is educate ourselves and our families. Do the research and remember, at the end of the day, the more natural the product, the better for the body. Humans have created many great things, but many damaging things too.

Do not join those who drink too much wine and gorge themselves on meat, for drunkards and gluttons become poor, and drowsiness clothes them in rags.
　　　　　　　 — *Proverbs 23: 19-21 (NIV)*

If You Don't Move It, You Lose It Or Add To It

We may be one of the laziest, most inactive societies in existence. We are unmotivated, out of shape and generally hesitant to try activities that would make us better. We gravitate to situations that require the least amount of effort. We have no energy, no motivation and bad attitudes to match.

You may be thinking to yourself, "I'm not lazy. I'm the busiest person I know." But here's the difference. Your day may be very busy, but how active are you? There is a huge difference between the two. Many Americans have a day that looks just like this...

- Wake up.
- Stand in the shower.
- Sit down and have breakfast/coffee/watch news.
- Stand up to dress.
- Sit down put shoes on.
- Stand up.
- Turn on the dishwasher and washing machine.
- Get in car.
- Sit and drive to work.
- Park as closely as possible to the door.
- Walk inside.
- Ride the elevator up 2 floors.
- Walk 20 feet to desk.
- Sit and work till lunch.
- Stand up and walk to elevator.
- Ride elevator down 2 floors.
- Walk to car.
- Ride to restaurant.
- Park as closely as possible.
- Walk inside.
- Sit down and eat.
- Walk to car.
- Ride back to work.
- Park as closely as possible.
- Walk inside.
- Ride elevator up 2 floors.
- Walk 20 feet to your desk.
- Sit at desk till 5.

Actions

- Walk 20 feet to elevator.
- Ride down 2 floors.
- Walk to car.
- Drive to pick up kids.
- Hit the drive-thru at Wendy's; eat in car.
- Drive to soccer practice.
- Sit on bleachers.
- Drive to Bible study.
- Sit to study.
- Attend choir practice.
- Sit to sing.
- Ride home.
- Walk inside.
- Sit down and complain about how long the day was and how tired we are.

This is a typical day for someone working in an office. There are more demanding, physically active jobs and hobbies out there, but overall we are very inactive. We choose the elevator or escalator over the steps, even when it's a single floor. We case a parking lot as long as it takes to get the closest spot. We use drive-up windows to get food, since we cannot spare the time to walk from the car and eat inside. And that cute little waitress that runs our food out to us and takes our money gets tipped for walking for us! We join gyms and waste our money by not using them. We take leisurely walks through the neighborhood with the dog, but complain if we are too cold or begin to sweat. We avoid activities that require physical exercise and that is costly to us in many ways. Exercise is one of the greatest tools for increasing our feelings of happiness. The lack of activity is stifling our world.

We were designed to move, to be active and support our bodies by keeping them strong. We should have adequate muscle mass to protect our bones and burn calories efficiently. We should keep our hearts strong by getting our heart rates up. Many years ago, people walked everywhere because that was their only option. What would we do without our cars? Did you know that the average American has enough body fat for 3 people? There was a time when that body fat may have saved someone's life, but we do not live in those times any more. We are not starving during a famine or long winter. Excess body fat will kill us, not keep us alive.

We must exercise to release the endorphins that make us feel good. Endorphins are part of a group of chemicals that naturally exist in the brain and help to alleviate pain and elevate a person's mood and spirit. They are also neurotransmitters produced by our brain during physical activity, sexual activity, joy, pain, laughter, massage and even during sleep. Endorphins play an important role in controlling our emotional behaviors like anxiety, fear, pleasure and pain. Endorphins have been compared to drugs like opium and morphine. The term "endorphin rush" has been adopted in popular speech to refer to feelings of exhilaration brought on by pain, danger, or other forms of stress, supposedly due to the influence of endorphins. Many runners have expressed a feeling of being "high" after a long run. This feeling is caused by endorphins.

We must exercise to keep our physical bodies in the best shape to enjoy the blessings awaiting our new thoughts and feelings. If we don't move it, we'll lose it. Mobility, flexibility, endurance and strength—all will be a struggle. The longer we go without exercising, the harder it is to get it back. If we don't move it, we'll add to it. Lack of activity mixed with all this crazy eating equals more pounds on our bodies. And those pounds are detrimental to our mental, emotional and physical health. It's not just about size; it's about health and being in the best bodies we can. Disease, poor health and poor self-image affect our thinking, which affects our feelings, which results in more damaging actions. Moving your body will help with all three.

> *Do you not know that your bodies are temples of the Holy Spirit, who is in you, whom you have received from God? You are not you own; you were bought at a price. Therefore honor God with your bodies.*
> — *1 Corinthians 6: 19-20 (NIV)*

Honoring God leads to His greatest blessings. That honor begins in our minds and continues with how we treat our body. God's promises of good health in mind and body are very clear.

> *Good friend, don't forget all I've taught you; take to heart my commands. They'll help you live a long, long time, a long life lived full and well. Don't lose your grip on Love and Loyalty. Tie them around your neck; carve their initials on your heart. Earn a reputation for living well in God's eyes and the eyes of the people. Trust God from the bottom of your heart; don't try to figure out everything on your own. Listen for God's voice in everything you do, everywhere you go; here's the one who will keep you on track. Don't assume that you know it all. Run to God! Run from the enemy! Your body will glow with health, your very bones will be great with life. Honor God with everything you own; give him the first and the best. Your barns will burst, you wine vats will brim over.*
> *Proverbs 3:1-12 (MSG)*

All that blessing begins with our thoughts and feelings. When we change our thoughts and feelings, we change our actions. We are able to use our positive attitudes and thankfulness to treat others as God would, making us conduits of blessings!

Other Addictions

I have absolutely no pleasure in the stimulants in which I sometimes so madly indulge. It has not been in the pursuit of pleasure that I have periled life and reputation and reason. It has been the desperate attempt to escape from torturing memories, from a sense of insupportable loneliness and a dread of some strange impending doom.

— Edgar Allan Poe

I know addiction. I'm a specialist. I've been addicted to many things and have just transferred that energy from one thing to another over the years. I have battled with alcohol, drugs, sex, shopping, food and people. The only thing I haven't tried is gambling, but that is strictly from a lack of access and knowledge. I'm very competitive, so learning poker could easily be the demise of my finances. We turn to our addictions to calm our nerves, dull our pain, numb ourselves up real good. These choices don't help us think clearly, feel good or behave better. Though they may seem like the perfect escape from reality, they often leave us more empty than we were to begin with.

Now I Lay Me Down To Sleep

For 15 years of my life, I had the most tortured dreams you could imagine. There were so many mornings when I awoke in utter terror. For several years, I took prescription medication to cure my depression. As a result, I battled severe night sweats and anxiety attacks in my sleep. The dreams would become so involved and detailed; they seemed so real. I would need to be awakened by someone else. It would take a good while to be coaxed back to reality.

Most of the dreams involved the death of my mother—not a funeral after she had died of natural causes. Her dream death would come after hours of being chased by large animals, running from tornados, swimming across lakes and rivers or climbing mountains. In most of the dreams I was responsible for everyone in the group, but felt the greatest need to save my mother. At the end of the dream, I would watch a tornado rip her out of my arms like we were in a Hollywood movie.

Her body would be shredded as I would scream out in failure and loss. The dreams got worse and worse each night.

In my nightmares, I saw myself killed several times. I saw myself shoot my daughter with a 12-gauge in our living room. I saw myself grieve the loss of my mother, daughter, father, so many people in my life. I saw myself cheated on and betrayed, trapped and taken advantage of. I even had a dream that I walked in on my mother having an affair with my daughter's father. The crazy images and journeys I took each night only contributed further to the darkness of my days. Fighting the demon of sleep became my only choice.

I tried to stay up as late as I could or take something to help me sleep through the night. The medication I was taking for my depression only seemed to intensify my dreams and it wasn't long until I decided to deal with the depression in other ways. I could not bear the sweats or the nightmares that haunted me every time I closed my eyes. This continued on and off for almost 15 years of my life.

It was one of my clients who initially helped me out with this problem. During a weight loss meeting, she told the story of David playing his harp to bring peace to Saul when he had bad dreams or was depressed. She encouraged us to lay our heads down at night and pray in thankfulness and expectation of a great night's sleep and a healing of the body and mind. I tried very hard to start praying for that very thing.

Then I read:

> *The more you worry, the more likely you*
> *are to have bad dreams....*
> — *Ecclesiastes 5:3* (MSG)

Wow. What a ground-breaking concept! That verse opened a whole new awareness for me. I was literally thinking myself into nightmares and hardship. In my dreams, I was living the pain and misery that I was thinking and feeling in my very own mind. It was showing up not only in the reality of my life, but in the subreality of my dreams. My subconscious mind, or hamster wheel, was continuing to stir this information at night. I was causing my own destruction.

As I lay in bed at night for all those years, I had thousands of negative thoughts spiraling through my mind. I worried about the bills, my financial state, my job, my relationships, death, pain, betrayal and loss. I fantasized about all these things when I went to bed at night. I experienced thoughts and feelings that would make anyone crazy. During this time of my life, I was in financial ruin. My boyfriend at the time was struggling with his own addictions, which had grave consequences on our relationship. I was always searching for and expecting the worst, right up to the very moment I shut my eyes.

It is crucial to change your bedtime routine. This is a simple yet life-changing principle. Be very aware of what you are feeding your hamster wheel before sleep. This is your time to run through your list of "Thank yous," a time to dream and hope. This is your time to prepare to come to God with joy as you lie in rest. This is your time to be sure that at least one-third of your day is spent in a positive realm.

What we put in the wheel before bed will turn for us all night long. I can tell you from hardcore experience it dictates the entire day, creating a spiral that feels like a nightmare from which we will never get a break.

Lie down to sleep in positive energy tonight. Why Wait?

One of Aesop's Fables

Paraphrased by
Gretchen Sortzi

Once upon a time there was a rabbit who boasted about how fast he was. He was constantly bragging to others and teasing those who were not. One day, an irate turtle answered back: "Who do you think you are? There's no denying you're swift, but even you can be beaten!" The rabbit squealed with laughter.

"Beaten in a race? By who? You? I bet there's nobody in the world that can win against me. Why don't you try?"

Annoyed by the cocky rabbit, the turtle accepted the challenge. A plan was made and they lined up to race the next morning. The rabbit was not intimidated by the turtle at all. He was confident he could wipe the floor with the turtle and curled up for a nap. The poor turtle was incredibly slow and by the time the rabbit awoke, the turtle was only halfway through the race. The rabbit ate some cabbages and smiled at the thought of the look on the turtle's face when he saw the rabbit speed by. He waited a little longer and then took off on the race. He leaped and bounded at a great rate, his tongue lolling, and gasping for breath. Just a little more and he'd be past that turtle. But as the rabbit reached the last bridge to the finish line, he tripped on a piece of wood sticking out, fell off the bridge and plummeted to his death. His last leap was just too late.

The turtle continued to walk along the path one step at a time. He slowly moved across that last bridge and was able to see the piece of wood sticking out, walk over it and continue forward. As he got to the final hill, fatigue and doubt tempted him to stop. The rabbit was already out of the race but the turtle continued on, with strength and focus leading the way. He crossed the finish line on the other side of the hill and felt joy and exhilaration. He had won the race and the victory was sweet. As the crowd looked on, he smiled and said, "Slow and steady wins the race."

Baby Steps

*D*o you remember that story? Probably not exactly as I have written it here, but I think you get the point.

Slow and steady definitely wins the race every time. That fable has a much deeper meaning in life. We all want to evolve and live at our highest selves. It naturally feels good and happiness can come easier. Any time we attempt change, we must move slowly. It's easier to institute small changes first and let them make permanent impressions on our lives. One small change at a time can lead to a big change in life. I've seen it myself.

I look at change like a swimming pool. No matter what temperature it is outside or how inviting the pool may look, that water is cold and there is no way I'm just jumping in. I don't even like to be splashed by accident when I'm working my way in. I'm generally one of those toe-toucher types, sticking a toe in first to feel the water. My toe leads me to believe further that the water is too cold and shocking to just jump into, and the best I can muster is putting my feet in on the first step. After a few minutes of standing in ankle-deep water, my feet send a message to my brain that they feel pretty good under there. I become a little less intimidated by the water and take the next step. The water is now to my knees and though I cringe for a moment taking that step, even more quickly, my brain receives the message that the water feels good. Before long I take another step and the water is now mid-thigh. The hardest step comes next, as the water will almost be up to my waist and I anticipate the dance I will do on my toes once I take that step. As I step down, I tiptoe all over the pool making faces and dreading the feeling of the water crossing my stomach and lower back. I dance around all while fighting a war in my mind over which feels better–the parts of my body now adjusted to the water or the parts waiting to go in. I realize in full consciousness that going under the water is my best and only option, but I fight it all the while. I finally suck up the courage and go the rest of the way into the water. As the water covers my shoulders, I quickly realize the final plunge was actually quite a relief. I move under the water, appreciating how amazing it feels and wondering why it took me so long just to get in. I appreciate my journey there and I appreciate my arrival even more.

This is absolutely true with people, places and things in our lives. If we want to change, we have to get our toes in the water. After one toe has adjusted, work your way into the water up to your ankles.

Move slowly down the steps as you are ready and able to do it. You'll find that as you change slowly, embracing the turtle in you, things will get easier. By the time you are halfway, you'll get a burst of fear. Being halfway means you are almost at the place of letting go. In fact, to really move forward all the way, to get what you want, that's exactly what you have to do. Let go. As you do, you will dive in and be free. There's a quote I love that says, "Being strong isn't always about holding on, but about knowing when to let go."

When we try to change, we reach a point where our old selves and our old behaviors will call us back. Once we reach halfway, once we dive in, we see that the water felt better all along. We'll have no desire to get out of the pool. When we do, we feel cold, lazy and hungry. We realize quickly as we exit that we need to get right back in. The outside no longer feels better. This is what we strive for.

Many of us have been more the jumping type; we just jump in and jump out, jump in and jump out. We make commitments on Monday and have already forgotten them by Thursday. We make New Year's resolutions that get broken on January 10. We jump on band wagon after bandwagon, never applying ourselves from start to finish. I know! I was that person. It's the little changes we make that add up over time and complete the bigger picture.

Don't be like the rabbit in the fable, either. We can't be on the fast track all the time. Real changes in life take time and effort—two things most of us lack. Life takes up all our time and our worries while struggles overtake our thought, preventing us from being the best selves we can be. Start slow and small to see the greatest and fastest rewards.

Awareness Is Everything

If we want to be something, anything, we have to acquire the most information we can and equip ourselves with the best tools. We need to armor ourselves with knowledge and routine. The more we learn and apply, the stronger we become.

For example, look at a great fisherman. If a fisherman wants to catch a big fish, he can't do so with a stick and some string. He buys the best pole he can afford. He gets the tastiest bait and drives the best boat he can. He wears the best fishing hat and his favorite fishing shirt. He probably even has the best little cooler holding the best sandwiches and the best beer. He is prepared and equipped to do well. He not only has the right equipment, but has studied his father and grandfather. He has taken years of experience to master his craft. He listened to the many lessons he was taught and applied them. When he got on the boat, he expected to catch fish, big fish. He had played movies in his mind of winning big prizes and hosting a huge fish fry. He thinks he is a success. He feels he is a success. The knowledge and tools he has MAKE him a success. He will catch big fish, lots of them. It works the same for anything you want to do or become.

If you are trying to create a healthier body, you have a lot of learning to do first. If you are going to eat right and exercise more, you need a guide. You need a true idea of what you are doing to increase your chances of success. As you learn, you become more aware and start making small changes that add up to big change. Before you know it, your knowledge and tools have transformed you to who and what you want to be.

When you change your thoughts, your feelings and the faith you have in yourself, you are well on your way. Match your intention with the awareness and tools to succeed and a new life will be yours. Whether you want to be a chef, a dancer, a carpenter, a parent or a marathon runner, when you change your thoughts and feelings, your actions fall in line to seal the deal. It's all up to you. Start creating the dream in your mind today.

An old Cherokee chief was teaching his grandson about life... "A fight is going on inside me," he said to the boy. "It is a terrible fight and it is between two wolves. "One is evil. He is anger, envy, sorrow, regret, greed, arrogance, self-pity, guilt, resentment, inferiority, lies, false pride, superiority, self-doubt and ego. "The other is good. He is joy, peace, love, hope, serenity, humility, kindness, benevolence, empathy, generosity, truth, compassion and faith. "This same fight is going on inside you and inside every other person, too." The grandson thought about it for a minute and then asked his grandfather, "Which wolf will win?" The old chief looked down in love and simply replied, "Whichever one you feed."

What a powerful story to wrap up this book. Each of us have that very same battle going on within. We are fighting on the inside and our pain and turmoil has in many ways become too much to bear. Our negative wolf has so much control it doesn't just dominate us with destruction, but it is also quick to reach out and bark misery at all those around us. When the negative wolf is in charge of your life, it has a dramatic impact on all those around you.

This is your day to cage the negative wolf. This is your moment to let the positive wolf take over your life so you may feel as Peter Pan describes. Freedom is only a thought away. I am praying each and every day for you. I am your dopamine, your personal cheerleader rooting for you. Let God, the God living within you, shine out to others. Thoughts lead to feelings, which lead to actions. Awareness is everything. ***Why Wait?***

Exercises And Meditations

Emotional Exercises

Empty The Chest

Exercise for Emotional Healing

Most of you have a large black treasure chest of unsettled emotions from your past, things you never completely grieved or dealt with. You've been storing these feelings since you were born. View this treasure chest as full and overflowing. Imagine how hard it is to keep the lid on it, because this in fact is true. These feelings are raging to come out and stay out. When they are dealt with and acknowledged, they will be gone. Use this exercise to help that process.

Feel

When an emotion hits you... feel it and let it sink in. We tend to fill up our large emotional chest instead. We tend to push the emotion down and try to hide from it or avoid it. If the emotion is not felt through and dealt with, it will return every time, and stronger too. When a feeling comes on ... feel it. Acknowledge that you're feeling it with words to yourself that may sound something like this... "I feel angry right now. Thanks for the info." By addressing the emotion, it will be felt, dealt with and moved out of your body, not stored in your "chest."

Use Your Triggers

Sit down and bring it on. Music, pictures, people, conversations, old letters, anything that triggers what you want to grieve about. Put on some music that encourages you to feel. Let the music take you wherever it will and go with it. If you feel like crying, cry. If you feel like laughing, laugh. Whatever the emotion, go with it and feel it. That will begin to clean out the chest and stop the cycle of storing it within you, which prevents us from reaching our greatest potential.

What You Give In, You Get Out

Fully give in to the feeling you are having. If you are feeling sad, don't know why and feel the urge to sob, then sob and do it to whatever level your body tells you to. Truly attempt to give in to the emotion with the intent of emptying it out of you. Each time we grieve, it gets easier to do again and there is less emotion left within you to deal with. Eventually we actually pass the emotion on and can heal.

What Is Blocked Will Block You

We believe we have healed from things, but we haven't, leaving us further and further from our goals. You may believe you have forgiven someone or something in your life. If feelings are still attached, you have not released it and it will keep you from your highest self.

Meditation for Visualization
— Peace Place —
Grass / Mountains

See your imagination as the most beautiful landscape you've ever seen. You can create whatever kind of landscape you want. Maybe enormous mountains surround you and you get lost looking at them. From a distance, the trees blend together to create a palette of color that takes your breath away. The trees are strong and magnificent. There is perfectly green grass as far as you can see, with gorgeous hills and expansive land. The various trees are tall and mighty, providing a great amount of shelter in their shade. It's a fantasy really, as close as you can get to the Garden of Eden. Flowers blanket a significant amount of the vision as well, all in vibrant colors that are stunning to the eyes. They shimmer in the sunlight that is always shining perfectly. There is a gentle breeze blowing, which provides the temperature of paradise. Butterflies dance around you and the feelings of peace and joy are the only ones you can express here.

You begin walking and realize you are wearing no shoes. You feel no fear. Each step you take, you take confidently, feeling a surge of energy from the perfect grass. You move gracefully and with great ease, each step feeling more and more like home. You feel comfortable and relaxed. You walk past a gorgeous lake. Two happy weeping willow trees stand on the opposite side. They are so inviting. You want to stop and sit for a moment, but you are compelled to keep moving to your dream place. You know you will be able come back and sit as long as you like. You continue to walk.

Within moments your dream place appears ahead of you. This dream place is a house of your choice. It can be an extremely large and elaborate house, in the woods, on a lake. A small log cabin may be more your style. Imagine all the details of your house from the outside. What do you see? Are there vehicles there? Do you see an image that makes you happy? Do you see fun toys and things you would want to have around the outside of your home to make you happy? Do you have a pool? Is there a gazebo? A garden? A waterfall? A rock wall? What makes your peace place inviting to you?

As you see the image of your peace place, you continue to walk. Each step you take brings you closer to your place, faster than you could ever move in reality.   Quickly, you are there. You walk onto your property and head toward the front door. Take the time to look around and appreciate all that is yours. Stand in front of the door and reach for the doorknob. A key appears in your dominant hand. You only need the key because it is your first visit to your peace place. Once it is unlocked, it will be open forever, so you may receive the blessings awaiting you inside. You use the key to open the door. As you turn the handle and push forward, the key disappears.

You step inside your peace place.

You close the door behind you and turn around to see in front of you a giant circular room. Along the round walls of the room are 7 doors. Each door is the same color, with a golden door handle and a plaque with gold writing. As you look up, you see a second floor of doors, then a third and a fourth. The stories continue as far up as you can see. You walk to your right, to the first door you see. The plaque on the door looks as if the letters have been dipped in real gold and hung on the door. The first sign reads... I am well. You don't need a key. You walk right in....

As you step inside the "I am well" room, an overwhelming feeling comes over you. You hear positive affirmations about yourself. I am generous. I am loved. I am beautiful. I am talented. I am limitless. I am abundant. Your gut begins to sizzle with a wonderful excitement and chills surge up your spine and out your arms to the very tips of your fingers. You see a small light within yourself and as you hear all these things, you begin to glow.

Within moments you are encompassed in light all around and within you. You feel complete, lacking nothing. You look around the room and see all your heart's desires. You are overcome with thankfulness and appreciation for all that is yours. You continue to repeat the mantra, "I am well" as you view everything in the room. You fall to your knees and throw your hands to the heavens. Tears come to your eyes as you shout, "I am well!"

Meditation for Visualization
— Peace Place — Beach

*I*magine the most beautiful landscape you've ever seen. You can create whatever kind of landscape you want. Perhaps you are most attracted to somewhere tropical. Imagine you can see white sandy beaches from your feet to the horizon. The ocean is a vast Caribbean blue and the temperature of the water is extremely inviting. The sky is majestic and there is beauty as far as you can see with enormous palm trees blowing in a perfect breeze. You can see extravagant houses ahead of you in the distance, perfectly positioned on the beach. It's a like a fantasy really, as close to paradise as you can get. Exotic flowers blanket a significant amount of the vision in vibrant colors stunning to your eyes. They shimmer in the perfect sunlight that is always shining. As the tide comes in you can feel the water across your feet and the salt water smell fills your senses. Butterflies begin to dance around you and the feeling of peace and joy is the only feeling you can express here.

You begin to walk feeling the warm sand beneath your feet. You feel no fear. Each step you take with confidence, feeling a surge of energy from the ocean at your side. You move gracefully and with great ease, each step feeling more and more like home. You feel comfort and relaxed. You walk past a magnificent turtle walking to the sea. Countless happy seashells blanket the beach. They are so picturesque. You want to stop and sit for a moment but you are propelled to keep moving to your dream place. You know you will be able come back and sit as long as you like. You continue to walk.

Within moments your dream place will appear ahead of you. Your dream place is a house of your choice. It can be an extremely large and elaborate house or a small cottage whatever is your style. Imagine all the details of your house from the out-side. What do you see? Are there vehicles there? Do you see an image that makes you happy? Do you see fun toys and things you would want to have around the outside of your home to make you happy? Do you have a pool? Is there a gazebo? A garden? A waterfall rock wall? What makes your peace place inviting to you?

As you see the image of your peace place you continue to walk. Each step you take brings you closer to your place, faster than you could ever move in reality. Quickly you are there. You walk onto your property and head toward the front door. Take the time to look around and appreciate all that is yours. Stand in front of your front door and reach for the doorknob. You feel a key appear in your dominant hand. You only need the key because it is your first time in your peace place. Once it is unlocked it will be forever, that you may receive the blessings awaiting you inside. You use the key to open the door. As you turn the handle and push forward the key disappears.

You step inside your peace place.

As you close the door behind you, you turn around to find in front of you a giant circular room. Along the round walls of the room are seven doors, each the same color with a gold door handle and a plaque with gold writing. As you look up you see a second floor of doors and a third and a fourth. The stories continue to go up as far as you can see. You walk to your right to the first door you. The plaque on the door looks as if the letters have been dipped in real gold and hung on the door. The first door reads... I am well. You don't need a key. You walk right in...

As you step inside the I am well room an over-whelming feeling comes over you. You begin to hear positive affirmations about yourself. I am generous. I am loved. I am beautiful. I am talented. I am limitless. I am abundant. Your gut begins to sizzle with a wonderful excitement and chills surge up your spine and out your arms to the very tip of your fingers. You see a small light within yourself and as you hear all these things you begin to glow.

Within moments you are encompassed in light all around and within you. You feel complete, lacking nothing. You look around the room and see all your hearts desires. You are overcome with thankfulness and appreciation for all that is yours. You continue to repeat the mantra, "I am well" as you view everything in the room. You fall to your knees and throw your hands to the heavens. Tears come to your eyes as you shout, "I am well."

Emotional Meditations

Chalk

The Archangel Raphael

St. Raphael is one of seven Archangels who stand before the throne of the Lord. He was sent by God and his name means "God Heals." He manages healers and healing for all of us. Ask this angel to help you with any pain you are dealing with—new, old, physical, or emotional. He is a master in all areas of healing. Be sure to stay in your awareness, as he will give you important information and knowledge and you never know where that message will come from. He brings with him an amazing emerald green light that shines from his halo. This is the color of healing and it will embrace and cover you completely. Be sure you are prepared to receive his healing. He will provide his care in the time he sees fit and if you are not in the right frame of positive thought, he may not be able to help you. Remember, thought is our paintbrush and we must support his efforts by having our minds focused on healing and positive energy. When asking any angel for help, always remember to give thanks when you have received. Blessings to you...

Meditation for Emotional Healing

ou open the door to your peace place, just like you always do, and as you walk inside, you see a beautiful green light radiating through the top of the building to a door on the sixth floor. It looks very much like a ray of sunshine, except is a gorgeous emerald green. You feel called to the light, so you start taking the steps, one floor at a time. You are not in a hurry. You just feel compelled to continue, each stair taking you further into a feeling of peace. As you step up onto the sixth floor, you can see the ray of green light vibrantly shining on the only door on the entire floor. As you walk toward the door, you look up and see the great healing angel Raphael floating from the heavens toward you. You see the emerald green light radiating from his halo as he gets closer to you. You feel a warm and cozy sensation as he lands in front of you, takes your hand and leads you to the door. He motions for you to open the door and nods "yes" to you.

You open the door and enter a large classroom. At no time do you feel fear, strange, funny or weird;

however the room is very cold. You feel safe, but you have no connection to the room. There is a single desk in the middle of the room and a single chair. On the chair is a jacket. Feeling chilly, you walk to the chair and put on the jacket. On the desk is a basket of chalk--white, yellow, pink, blue and green. You select a piece of chalk. As you look around the room, you notice that all of the walls are green chalkboards. You can write all over the walls, anywhere you want.

You suddenly feel overwhelmed with ideas of what to write. You write down all the situations and experiences that created guilt or pain in your life. You write about hurts from your childhood, scars from bad relationships and betrayals, times of loss and pain, moments when you questioned, guilt from mistakes. You write about everything that ever hurt you or pained you. You see all the guilt you hold in your heart. You see names, places and times in your life. You write everything on the wall that you can think of.

Anything that is haunting you is now covering all 4 walls. Your hand aches, as you've been writing a long time. You are very tired. You feel like you need to sit down. The energy and momentum you had while writing immediately dissipates and you feel as if you will fall on the floor. The weakness in your body comes on strong and fast and as you struggle to catch yourself against the desk, the emerald green ray of light breaks through the door and covers you. As your body is completely covered by the light, you feel energized and are able to stand up. Once you are on your feet, a ray of perfect white light bursts through the ceiling onto your head. It moves through your whole body, shooting out your hands and down through your feet. The white light wraps itself in the green light that was already pouring into you. Your arms are outstretched as you feel a sensation moving from your toes slowly up your entire body. As the feeling almost leaves your head, you look to the sky and see Jesus smiling down at you. You feel His love so powerfully through his light that you are instantly filled up. You look to Raphael and see he is smiling. He reaches out his hand to you again and says, "You have been healed. Do you believe?" The feeling of wholeness and oneness with spirit makes your answer simple. You say, "I am healed." As you utter the words, the room literally disappears from around you and you are standing back at the entrance to your peace place, cleansed and ready to manifest at the level you deserve.

Drop the Bags

Premeditation Preparation

*B*efore beginning the meditation, prepare your bags. You will create a bag or a suitcase for any person or responsibility you have in your life. Include any person or thing that causes you to worry. The look and condition of each bag represents how you truly feel about those things. For example, if you have a spouse or partner, you definitely need a bag for them. Some of you may see a clean, new, easy-to-tote suitcase with new wheels that rolls along with you in stride, while others may see a suitcase with a beat-up exterior and broken wheels that constantly needs to be dragged along. You might also have a bag for your children (one for each), parents, job, friendships, church, sports team or anything in your life that causes you worry or for which you have responsibility.

Most important, you have a giant bag, taller than you, that follows behind you. It's a black trash bag and inside it are all the negative emotions you have experienced or are faced with at any given time. It has been filling up for as many years as you've been alive. It holds shame, guilt, hurt, pain, judgment, betrayal, regret and grudges you hold against others. It is filled with nothing that serves the "you" that you truly are. When you have formed a mental image of your bags, begin the meditation.

Meditation for Emotional Healing

Sit down in a place where you can be at peace for a few minutes. Close your eyes and imagine yourself in darkness. You feel nothing with you or around you. It is quiet and dark. Suddenly you see a white light ahead of you and you walk toward it. It is hard for you to move, as if you are weighed down by something or someone. You work hard to get to the light and as you get closer, the light continues to intensify. Within a few minutes, you are standing in front of a large mirror, big enough to see your entire self. All around you are bags—in your arms, on the ground, on your back, in front, behind and beside you. The giant black bag looms behind you and you can feel how heavy it is. It is impossible to carry. You feel dread at the thought of having to pick it up.

As you look at yourself in the mirror and see all the bags piled around, you realize just how much weight they make altogether. They are impossible to carry for anyone. You feel the emotional burden that each one represents and as the feeling of weight intensifies, you begin to feel faint. One by one, the bags are placed in your arms and on top of you. You cannot pick them up fast enough or balance them all. You take a deep breath and drop all the bags.

As each bag hits the floor, you feel the release of the attachment, burden, responsibility, worry. A feeling of release of all that you carry along with you surges through your body. You turn around to face the large bag behind you. As you look the bag over, a bright white light surges through the sky into your body. You are filled with the white light. A superhuman strength comes over you and you push the large bag away from you. You use all your force to push the bag into the darkness until you cannot see it any more. Positive emotions flood your body as you feel the power of this victory. You look back to the mirror and offer yourself congratulations for forgiving yourself, for letting go and releasing the bags.

Slowly walk away from the mirror, leaving the remaining bags on the ground where you were standing. Walk away until the mirror and bags get smaller and smaller and you are back in the darkness. Take a deep breath. Be thankful for your release. Open your eyes. You are cleansed and ready to move forward.

After Your First Experience....

Walk into the visualization next time carrying your bags with you, now that you have created them. Be sure to create a new bag to represent any new things that have come into your life. Each time you do this exercise, it should get easier to release. Be sure to allow the large black emotional trash bag to get smaller and smaller until you have deleted that bag from your life.